Daily *warm-ups*

EARTH SCIENCE

J. WESTON
WALCH
PUBLISHER
Portland, Maine

1   2   3   4   5   6   7   8   9   10
ISBN 0-8251-4362-4
Copyright © 1992, 2002
J. Weston Walch, Publisher
P.O. Box 658 • Portland, Maine 04104-0658
www.walch.com
Printed in the United States of America

The *Daily Warm-Ups* series is a wonderful way to turn extra classroom minutes into valuable learning time. The 180 quick activities—one for each day of the school year—review, practice, and teach earth-science topics. These daily activities may be used at the very beginning of class to get students into learning mode, near the end of class to make good educational use of that transitional time, in the middle of class to shift gears between lessons—or whenever else you have minutes that now go unused. In addition to providing students with fascinating earth-science activities, they are a natural path to other classroom activities involving critical thinking.

Daily Warm-Ups are easy-to-use reproducibles—simply photocopy the day's activity and distribute it. Or make a transparency of the activity and project it on the board. You may want to use the activities for extra-credit points or as a check on critical-thinking skills and problem-solving skills.

However you choose to use them, *Daily Warm-Ups* are a convenient and useful supplement to your regular lesson plans. Make every minute of your class time count!

What's in a Hypothesis?

Here are two hypotheses about the origin of the earth.

Collision Theory

The sun collided with another star. Hot material from the collision was set in rotation. As the hot material cooled, small planetary bodies formed. These bodies joined together, grew in size, and formed planets.

Tidal Theory

A star passed the sun, causing a gigantic tide. The tide broke loose from the sun as globs of hot, molten material. The globs cooled, condensed, and formed the planets.

Make a sketch to illustrate one of the theories.

It's All Greek to Me

Of the six names listed in the box below, see if you can identify three scientists who lived in ancient Greece. Unscramble the clues to solve the puzzle.

1.  + 🪓 + i + **na** (backwards) + [or] _d_ _e_ _r_ (how you get food at a restaurant).

2. **To** (backwards), + _l_ _e_ [t] (word meaning *allow*) + + **a.** (area where hand bends without the *w*)

3. _p_ _i_ _c_ [k] (word meaning *select* or *choose*) + e + _u_ _s_ (you and me) + sounds like *you* + 18th letter of the alphabet.

Anaxagoras	Empedocles
1 Anaximander	3 Epicurus
2 Aristotle	Xenophanes

2

It Takes a Lot of Crust

About 14 elements make up the earth's crust. **Silicon** (Si) comprises about 28 percent of the earth's crust. Another important element constitutes almost 47 percent of the crust. What is that element?

Read the three clues to help you find the answer.

Clue #1. Two of its letters often appear as unknowns in algebra.

X and Y

Clue #2. It can be generated from mercuric oxide.

Clue #3. It is responsible for nearly 50 percent of the weight of the earth's crust.

The important element is Oxegyn .

Outer Layer

Earth is the planet we live on. Salt water covers about 71 percent of the surface of the earth. The crust covers the solid, rocky part of the earth. Scientists use an 11-letter word to refer to the solid part of the earth. What is that word?

To find out, unscramble the underlined letters and place them in the blank spaces below.

t̲hrust fault   min e̲ral   glaci e̲r   volcan o̲

mountai̲n   h̲ill   s̲oaps̲tone

The word is l i t h o s p h o r e .

(handwritten notes: tho i / there oihsp / litho / sphece)

The Core of the Problem

Unscramble the terms in the left column and place them in the spaces below. Then match the **description** in the right column with the **layer of the earth** in the left column. (Write the letter of the description in the space next to the term's number.)

Layer of the Earth

_b_ 1. rinen reco

inner core

_d_ 2. usctr

crust

_a_ 3. entmla

Mantle

_c_ 4. oretu roec

Outer core

Description

a. next to crust, heavy rocks—iron, magnesium, silicon compounds

b. center of earth, made of Fe and Ni

c. about 2,100 kilometers thick, liquid iron and nickel

d. outermost section of the outer part of the earth

5

On Firm Ground

Fill in the blanks with a term that rhymes with the words in parentheses.

Scientists say the earth has a crust of solid _rock_ (knock, clock).

The mantle lies between the crust and the _core_ (floor, snore).

The _dense_ (fence, sense), metallic core makes up the innermost _____ (heart, start) of the _Earth_ (birth, worth).

Circle the letters that spell the name of an item or object known or believed to be present in each of the following layers of the earth. The answer is hidden in the series of letters. There is only one answer for each series of letters.

CRUST—M I G O I L C A W T A E R O P L E I W

MANTLE—B U G M O L D I R O N I N S E C T A P

CORE—D I M E N I C K E L W A T E R A N T O

Who Studies the Earth?

A scientist who studies the origin, history, and structure of the solid earth and the processes that shape it has a special name. This individual knows a lot about min<u>e</u>ra<u>l</u>s, r<u>o</u>cks, moun<u>tai</u>ns, <u>g</u>laciers, <u>g</u>r<u>o</u>und water, and so on.

To reveal the special name, unscramble the underlined letters in the words above and fill in the blanks.

This person is known as a _geologist_.

7

Earth Observation 1

How many of the earth's objects or features can you identify? Use the clues to help you find them.

Hint: The features are found on the earth's surface.

Earth Features   **Clues**

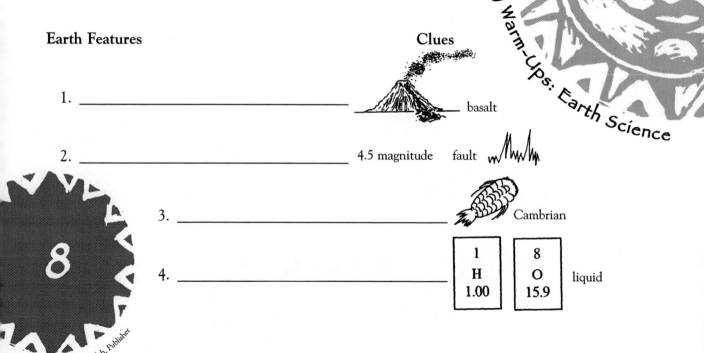

1. _____ basalt

2. _____ 4.5 magnitude   fault

3. _____ Cambrian

4. _____   liquid

8

Earth Observation 2

Use the clues listed below to help you locate four of the earth's features found on the bottom of the sea.

Undersea Features   **Clues**

1. abyssal _____

?

ocean basin

2. _____

shelf

?

3. _____

4. _____

Earth Observation 3

How many of the earth's features or scientific instruments can you identify? Use the symbols, letters, sketches, and phrases to help you find answers. Write your answer in the space provided.

1. Shake, rattle, and roll from earthquakes— sounds like vault.

   _____

2. An instrument to study stars planets

   a Galileo discovery   two lenses

   _____

3. A cave feature   calcium carbonate   roof of a cave   dripping H_2O

   _____

4. "Exploding" water   opposite of *gal*, opposite of *madam*

   _____

5. Earth's surface   letter c, plus what happens when Fe combines with O_2

   _____

10

Plate Fate

Lithospheric plates move constantly. Three major geological events result from plate movement. The paired words below rhyme with the name of each geological event.

Use the rhyming clues to identify each major geological event. Write the answers in the empty spaces.

1. worth snakes　　　　＿＿＿＿＿＿＿＿＿＿

2. titanic deductions　　＿＿＿＿＿＿＿＿＿＿

3. fountain gilding　　　＿＿＿＿＿＿＿＿＿＿

Soil 1

What is made of a mixture of weathered rocks, decomposed plants and animals, and bacteria? The answer, of course, is **soil.**

The upper layer of soil is known as topsoil. **Humus,** dark material produced from decaying organic matter, makes up part of the topsoil.

Fill in the spaces below with the names of any plants and animals likely to die, decompose, and turn into humus. Use the letters **H, M,** and **S** as the first letters of each name.

H _____ _____
        animal   plant

U

M _____ _____
        animal   plant

U

S _____ _____
        animal   plant

H _____ _____
        animal   plant

U

M _____ _____
        animal   plant

U

S _____ _____
        animal   plant

Soil 2

A **soil profile** is a vertical section of three distinct layers, known as **soil horizons.** Over time, weathered rocks—made up of different materials—form different colors and textures in each horizon.

Use the letter groups in Horizons A, B, and C to form the names of the materials that comprise each horizon. Write the names in the empty spaces inside the soil profile.

Soil Profile

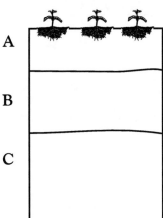

A

B

C

bedrock

Horizon

A

hu	sa	ro
ots	nd	mus

HINT: 3 words

B

cl	lt	si
nd	sa	ay

HINT: 3 words

C

wea	ck	bed
red	the	ro

HINT: 2 words

13

Earth Terms

Six of the terms in the box relate to the study of the earth. Match them with their descriptions by writing the term in the space to the right of the description.

astrologer	paleontologist
cardiologist	petrologist
cartographer	physiologist
geologist	radiologist
hydrologist	seismologist

Description	Related Term
1. A person who makes maps	_____
2. A person who studies earthquake phenomena	_____
3. A person who studies rocks	_____
4. A person who studies fossils	_____
5. A person who studies the waters of the earth	_____
6. A person who studies the earth	_____

Earth to Moon

The earth and the moon work together to produce certain earth events. Two of these events are named in the word find puzzle below. You may find the answers by reading up, down, forward, backward, or diagonally.

Circle your answers.

```
S   A   C   J   A   I   E
O   E   I   U   L   S   I
L   A   D   P   P   M   O
U   D   N   I   W   A   T
A   E   L   T   T   R   U
B   C   G   E   A   S   L
E   V   I   R   O   A   P
```

15

Be Specific!

Specific gravity is the ratio obtained by comparing the density of a substance with the density of water. Anything with a specific gravity greater than 1 (the specific gravity of water) will sink.

The formula for specific gravity is

$$\text{specific gravity} = \frac{\text{weight of substance in air}}{\text{weight in air} - \text{weight in water}}$$

Use the formula to determine which of the three substances below—A, B, or C—has the highest specific gravity.

Substance	Weight in air (g)	Weight in water (g)
A	22.5	15.5
B	19.2	15.2
C	15.0	6.0

Calculate the average specific gravity of all three substances. What do you notice?

16

A Dense Moment

Margaret said to Jenny, "My object is more dense than your object."

"No way," snapped Jenny. "My object has a mass of 134 grams and a volume of 42 cubic centimeters."

"Oh, yeah?" replied Margaret. "My object has a mass of 206 grams with a volume of 72 cubic centimeters."

Which girl, Margaret or Jenny, wins the argument?

Hint: Density equals mass divided by volume, or $D = \frac{M}{V}$.

17

Spin Zone

An object traveling in a circle behaves *as if* it is subjected to an outward force. But that force, known as **centrifugal force,** does not actually exist! It just seems real to the object being rotated.

In other words, centrifugal force is the *apparent* pull away from the center when a body moves in a curve. An example would be Earth orbiting the sun. Centrifugal force seems to make the earth fly away into space. Fortunately, the sun's gravitational force pulls the earth toward its center.

Fill in the blanks below with letters that complete the examples of things under the influence of centrifugal force.

18

1. a sp _ _ d s _ at _ r making a quick t _ rn (7 words)

2. a fast - m _ v _ ng ra _ e car turning ov _ r and _ _ er (8 words)

3. a p _ rs _ _ s _ in _ i _ g a _ ei _ ht on a r __ p _ (8 words)

4. a r _ l _ er _ k _ _ er rounding a _ ur _ e (6 words)

5. a wh _ _ li _ g ba _ _ e _ in _ (3 words)

6. a s _ i _ ni _ _ t _ p (3 words)

A Force, of Course

Gravity is a force of attraction between objects and the earth.

List seven objects commonly found in many classrooms that are affected by gravity.

```
            G _ _ _ _
_ _ _ _ _   R
    _ _ A _ _
        V _ _ _
_ _ _ _ I _
        T _ _ _ _ _ _
        Y _ _
```

19

Call It Stuff

Matter is anything that has mass and takes up space. In a word, it's stuff.

The scrambled words on the left are examples of mass. Items on the right are measures of matter. Unscramble each mass term and write it in the space provided. Then draw a line connecting each of your mass terms with an example of matter.

Mass		Measure of Matter
1. otn	_____	a. Weight of a paper clip
2. armg	_____	b. Asteroid—2,000 pounds
3. glimokra	_____	c. Candy—2.2 pounds

20

Daily Warm-Ups: Earth Science

Mostly Elementary

A chemical **element** is a simple substance that cannot be broken down into simpler substances. An element contains only one kind of atom.

Look at a **periodic table.** Use the chemical letter symbols to help you find and circle the hidden letter symbols of elements in the sentences below.

Hint: The first letter of a chemical symbol is *always* a capital letter.

1. As luck would have it, Connie won again! _____ _____

2. Nobody came to Francine's party. Francine said, "I'm through giving parties."

   _____ _____ _____

3. "What month follows July?" asked Bert. "August . . . duh," replied Bert's younger brother, Carl.

   _____ _____ _____ _____

4. "Are you going to the dance tonight?" asked Mona. "Nah," replied Tracy. "Not me."

   _____ _____ _____

5. Veronica participates in after-school athletics. She plays basketball and soccer.

   _____ _____

21

Combining Matter

Elements can combine chemically to form **compounds.**

Examples: $NaCL$ = salt, SiO_2 = sand, CO_2 = carbon dioxide

Daily Warm-Ups: Earth Science

Use the elements and clues to help you assemble six different compounds below.

Elements	Clues	Compound
1. H, N, O	H (1), N (1), O (3)	_____
		nitric acid
2. H, S, O	H (2), S (1), O (4)	_____
		sulfuric acid
3. Fe, S	Fe (1), S (2)	_____
		iron disulfide
4. Al, O	Al (2), O (3)	_____
		aluminum oxide
5. H, O	H (2), O (2)	_____
		hydrogen peroxide
6. Cu, S, O	Cu (1), S (1), O (4)	_____
		copper sulfate

22

What do you notice about five of the compounds? _____

Miniature Matter 1

Atoms are the basic units of matter. Atoms are composed of smaller particles known as **protons, electrons,** and **neutrons.** Read each numbered statement below.

Shade in the number of each true statement to reveal an element that is abundant in bananas and orange juice.

1. Protons have a negative charge.

2. Protons have a positive charge.

3. Protons are the heaviest subatomic particle.

4. Protons are located in the nucleus.

5. Protons were discovered by Dr. Proteus.

5	1	4	1	3	4	3	1
3	1	2	3	2	3	3	5
5	3	2	4	5	5	3	3
3	3	4	2	5	5	3	5
5	3	2	5	2	3	3	1
5	1	4	1	3	4	1	3

23

Miniature Matter 2

Atoms are the basic units of matter. Atoms are composed of smaller particles known as **protons, electrons,** and **neutrons.**

Read each numbered statement. In the puzzle below, shade in the number of each true statement to reveal the chemical symbol for the lightest of all elements.

1. Electrons are nearly weightless subatomic particles.
2. Electrons can often be found inside the nucleus.
3. Electrons carry a negative electric charge.
4. Electrons are seldom found at different energy levels.
5. Electrons are moving charged particles.

2	4	1	4	3	4	2
4	4	5	2	1	2	4
4	2	1	3	5	4	2
2	4	3	4	3	2	2
4	2	1	2	3	2	4

Miniature Matter 3

Atoms are the basic units of matter. Atoms are composed of smaller particles known as **protons, electrons,** and **neutrons.**

Read each numbered statement below. In the puzzle below, shade in the number of each true statement about neutrons to reveal the symbol of the basic element in coal.

1. Discovered by Dmitry Mendeleyev.
2. Neutrons are the lightest of all subatomic particles.
3. Neutrons are subatomic particles with no charge.
4. Neutrons are found inside the nucleus.
5. Neutrons have six times the mass of a proton.

2	2	4	3	4	3	2	1
5	1	3	5	1	2	5	1
2	5	4	5	2	5	1	5
1	2	3	1	1	2	2	5
1	5	4	4	4	3	5	1

Changing Matter 1

A **physical change** occurs when a substance changes in size, shape, or form with no change in composition. In other words, the chemical makeup stays the same.

List six ways you can physically change a new bar of soap using your thumbnail, a sharpened pencil, and a table knife.

1. _____

2. _____

3. _____

4. _____

5. _____

6. _____

26

Changing Matter 2

A **chemical change** occurs when one substance becomes a different substance—with *different chemical properties*.

Example: Burning paper gives off heat, light, and smoke. A thin layer of ashes remains behind.

In each of the following examples, place a checkmark in the space beside the number if you think a *chemical* change occurs.

___ 1. Maria bends a penny with a hammer.

___ 2. Marcus breaks a plastic spoon into eight pieces.

___ 3. Lightning strikes an area containing sandy soil. Some of the soil turns into glass.

___ 4. Joan evaporates 200 milliliters of water from a 1-liter flask.

___ 5. Devon pours vinegar over Daniel's container of baking soda.

___ 6. Juanita stretches a rubber band until it breaks.

27

A Solid Start

The **solid state** of matter takes up a definite volume and has a definite shape.

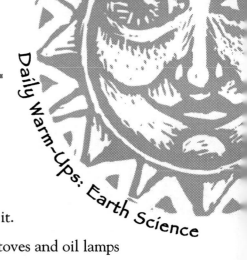

Use the hint list below to help you unscramble the six numbered items. Then write the unscrambled word in the space provided. Circle the numbers of the three examples of solid matter.

Item	Hint List
1. racih _____	You can sit on it.
2. ekneerso _____	A fuel for oil stoves and oil lamps
3. ncorab _____	Found in coal; atomic number 6
4. etasm _____	A power source for turbine engines
5. arleitmwe _____	Clear; calcium hydroxide
6. rrebub _____	Elastic; flexible and waterproof

28

Time to Expand

Matter in a **gaseous** state has no definite shape and expands to fill its container.

Circle the five terms below that are associated with gas.

steam	vapor	crystal
air	magnesium	sodium
oxygen	copper	helium

What do the other *uncircled* words have in common?

29

Free Flow

Matter in a **liquid** state takes up a definite volume but has no definite shape. Liquid molecules move more freely than solid molecules, but less freely than gas molecules. **Cohesion** is the force that causes liquid molecules to stick together.

Add letters to the letters in the word COHESION to identify eight different liquids. (There's a clue or two in the right column.)

	Clues
_ _ _ C _	pour on food for flavor
_ _ O _ _	contains plasma
H _ _ _ _	sweet, syrupy
_ _ _ E _	has two hydrogen atoms
S _ _ _ _	salty secretion
_ I _ _	comes from mammary glands
O _ _	greasy, combustible fuel
_ _ _ N	condensed vapor

30

Matter Model

Scientists make **models** to explain difficult concepts—and sometimes to make predictions. A model for an oxygen molecule might look like this:

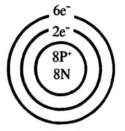

$6e^-$
$2e^-$
$8P^+$
$8N$

Design a model for each of these elements: carbon (atomic number 6) and sodium (atomic number 11).

31

Moving Matter

The earth produces enough energy to move huge masses of land. Some scientists believe **convection currents** within the earth's mantle cause land to shift, creating volcanoes, undersea ridges, faults, and trenches. Convection currents develop as melted rocks move upward in the earth's mantle.

What produces the heat necessary to melt rocks in the earth's mantle? Use the clue to discover the two-word answer in the scattered letters.

Clue: Circle every other letter to put it together.

c r e a i d b i m o t a l c e t g i y v x e

First Word __ __ __ __ __ __ __ __ __ __ __

t e o l d e k m p e z n f t q s

Second Word __ __ __ __ __ __ __ __

The answer is __ __ __ __ __ __ __ __ __ __ __ __ __ __ __ __ __ __ __.

32

Mineral Mix

Minerals are nonliving natural substances found in the earth. Minerals can mix together to form rocks. For example, the minerals mica, hornblende, quartz, and plagioclase feldspar combine to form granite.

Use the symbols listed below to show how minerals are scattered through granite rock. The figure below represents a granite boulder. Go ahead and have fun filling in the figure with triangles, squares, circles, and pluses.

■ mica
● hornblende
+ plagioclase feldspar
▲ quartz

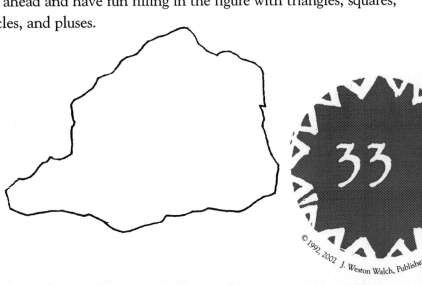

Twelve Minerals

Do you know that two chemical elements, oxygen and silicon, make up more than half of the earth's outer crust? In fact, 99 percent of the earth's crust is made up of only 12 elements. These elements combine as rock-forming minerals.

Twelve minerals of the rock-forming group are listed below. Write the missing letters in the spaces provided to complete the name for each mineral. Refer to the periodic table, if necessary.

1. ____ mph ___ b ___ le

2. p ___ ro ___ ene

3. ___ eld ___ p ___ r

4. mu ___ co ___ it ___

5. bi ___ t ___ te

6. ___ liv ___ ne

7. ch_____ o ____ ite

8. ____ uar ___ z

9. se___ pen ___ ___ ne

10. t ___ lc

11. st ___ lbi ___ e

12. an ___ lcite

34

Silicate Shuffle

A **silicate** mineral contains silicon (Si) combined with oxygen (O), plus some other element or elements. Silicates make up more than 90 percent of the minerals found in the earth's crust.

Use the letters, words, and numbers to help you write the chemical formulas for each silicate below.

1. quartz   S + eye, O two _____

2. zircon   Z + are, es aye, O fore _____

3. rhodonite   M + n, sigh , O trio _____

4. potassium feldspar   kay, A + L, Si (12–9), O ate _____

35

© 1992, 2002 J. Weston Walch, Publisher

Mineral Beauty Contest

Minerals come in various sizes and shapes.

Read the four descriptions below and underline the mineral that best matches each description.

1. "Very heavy, cubelike specimen with a metallic luster"
   halite   galena   garnet   quartz

2. "Soft, cubelike specimen with a salty taste."
   sulfur   calcite   halite   galena

3. "Crystals occur in an almost endless variety of forms and combinations. A fairly soft mineral."
   halite   fluorite   quartz   calcite

4. "May be colorless, glassy; produces six-sided crystals."
   calcite   quartz   halite   fluorite

Extra: What do all of these minerals have in common?

A Tough Mineral

A mineral's ability to resist scratching is known as **hardness.**
Gypsum is a soft mineral that can be scratched by quartz. Therefore,
quartz is harder than gypsum.

Read the statements below. Then determine from the information
which of the minerals is hardest.

Mineral X is scratched by minerals Y and Z.

However, minerals L and S will not scratch mineral X.

Interestingly, mineral Y can scratch minerals Z and T.

Mineral T can scratch mineral Z.

Mineral _____ is the hardest.

37

Which Crystal Is It? 1

Identify the mystery **crystal.** Place your answer in the space provided. You'll have to unscramble the seven circled letters to discover the name of the mystery crystal.

1. The chemical symbol for argon: ◯ r.

2. A yellow, sour fruit: ◯ emon.

3. The opposite of rare: ◯ ommon.

4. Tin, copper, and sodium are examples: El ◯ ments.

5. The results of two or more elements combining: ◯ ompounds.

6. The opposite of positive: Negat ◯ ve.

7. Able to bend and spring back: Elas ◯ ic.

Mystery crystal: _____

38

Which Crystal Is It? 2

Identify the mystery **crystal.** Place your answer in the space provided. You'll have to unscramble the six missing letters to discover the name of the mystery crystal.

1. A large mass of ice and snow   g l a c i e __

2. The way a mineral splits   c l e __ v a g e

3. An erupting hot spring   g __ y s e r

4. A hollow sphere lined with crystals   __ e o d e

5. An intrusion of igneous rock   p l u __ o n

6. A zone of Earth rock   m a __ t l e

Mystery crystal: _____

39

Three Unique Minerals

Some **minerals** have special characteristics—for example, yellow color (sulfur), double refraction (calcite), salty taste (halite).

Use the hints below to identify the three minerals with special properties. You'll find the answers in a list of 12 minerals below the table.

Mineral	Hints
	Very heavy; a liquid metal at room temperature
	Soft, highly malleable; the most sought after mineral
	Brilliant metallic luster; cubed crystals; specific gravity about 7.5

apatite	diamond	topaz	barite
quartz	galena (lead ore)	tourmaline	mercury
talc	gold	serpentine	fluorite

Hail to Halite

Halite, rock salt, is sodium chloride, NaCl. It is soft, has a low specific gravity, and forms cube-shaped crystals.

In the following story, circle the letters, words, and parts of words that relate to the above description of halite.

Mr. Morcuber teaches earth science at Reynolds Middle School. When he asked his third-period earth-science class to name three igneous rocks, Nadine C. Leiter belted out, "Granite, basalt, and obsidian." Crystal Lecuben, Nadine's friend, smiled and whispered, "You big show-off."

41

Fun With Mineral Names

Say the name of each mineral listed below, on the left. Then find a phrase in the column on the right that relates to the sound of the mineral's name. Write the letter of that phrase next to the mineral's name. Use each phrase only once. The first one is done for you.

Mineral	Related Phrase
1. spinel _d_	a. six-legged critter
2. galena __	b. wild canine; carnivorous
3. witherite __	c. large poisonous snake
4. antimony __	d. backbone; vertebrae
5. wulfenite __	e. to dry up; shrivel
6. serpentine __	f. a girl

42

Heavy Mineral

Specific gravity refers to the ratio of the mass of one substance to the mass of an equal volume of water. For example, hematite, an iron ore, has a specific gravity of 5.3. Therefore, hematite is 5.3 times heavier than an equal volume of water.

$$\text{specific gravity} = \frac{\text{weight of substance in air}}{\text{weight in air} - \text{weight in water}}$$

Example: Mineral A's dry weight = 58 grams, and its wet weight = 30 grams. Then

Specific gravity = 58 ÷ (58 – 30)

Specific gravity = 58 ÷ 28 = 2.07

Problem: Is the following statement true or false?

Mineral X has a higher specific gravity than Mineral Y.

Mineral X: dry weight = 32 g; wet weight = 25 g

Mineral Y: dry weight = 20 g; wet weight = 15.5 g

43

Rock 'n' Riddle

Look at the diagram of a rocky mountain and the eight scattered words within it. Combining the first letter of each word reveals something about the rocky mountain. Put the letters in the correct order to find the answer.

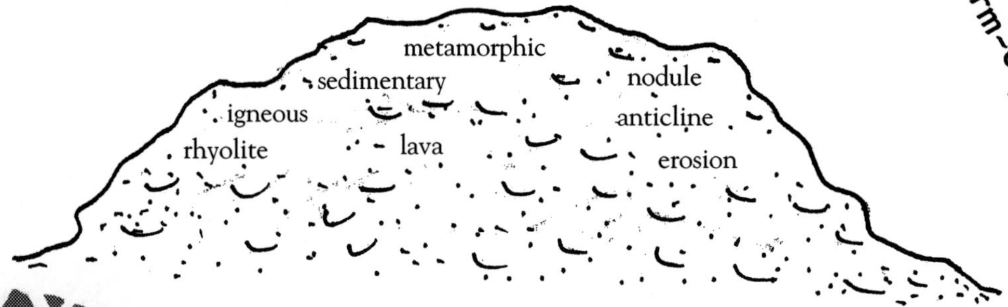

metamorphic

sedimentary

igneous

nodule

anticline

rhyolite

lava

erosion

Answer: _____

44

Rock to Rock

The **rock cycle** produces new rocks from old ones. Recycling occurs at a very slow pace. Old rocks at the earth's surface weather and form sediments. The sediments are buried and heated under tremendous pressure. The pressure causes some rock to recrystallize into new rock. In time, the new rock may appear on the earth's surface.

What energy source causes new rock to reach the earth's surface? Combine the letters in HATE, INN, and LATER to fill in the blanks.

Hint: The letters in INN and LATER combine to form the first of the two words.

The earth's __ __ __ __ __ __ __ __   __ __ __ __

45

Rock Three

The **rock cycle** acts like a magician, changing one type of rock into another, then turning it back into its original form.

What three types of rock have gone through the cycle several times during the earth's history? Fill in the blanks below with the missing letters and use the clues to help you identify each rock type.

Type 1. __ __ + a U.S. coin + n + a solid particle found in tobacco smoke + y

_____

46

Type 2. __ __ + three-letter prefix meaning *new* + objective case of *we*

_____

Type 3. prefix meaning change in form + _ + a conjunction introducing the second of two possibilities + __ __ __ __

_____

Puzzling Magma

Magma from deep inside the earth is the source of igneous rock.

Look at the sketch below. The letters can be combined to form the names of four different kinds of magma. Identify these kinds of magma that occur before a volcano erupts. Write the letters of each answer in the spaces provided.

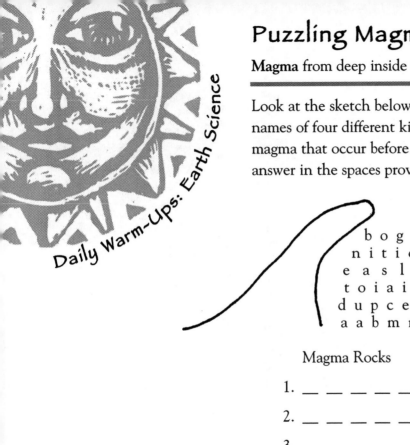

```
        b o g
      n i t i o
    e a s l b
    t o i a i n
    d u p c e m
    a a b m r s
```

Magma Rocks

1. _ _ _ _ _ _ _

2. _ _ _ _ _ _ _

3. _ _ _ _ _ _ _ _

4. _ _ _ _ _ _

47

What Rock Is It? 1

Use the poetic information provided below to identify the
igneous rock.

Fire-grained and glassy,

So very, very classy.

Yet the conchoidal fracture

Adds beauty to the rapture.

Would you like one more hint? If so, then you should know the answer
is among the igneous rocks listed below.

granite	pumice
tuff	obsidian
felsite	rhyolite
basalt	scoria

The igneous rock is _____.

What Rock Is It? 2

Use the poetic information provided below to identify the **igneous** rock.

> Some lava may be hotter,
>
> But this one floats on water.
>
> And when you need to shine or grind,
>
> This is the rock to keep in mind.
>
> Here are two more hints:
>
> It has ice in it, but the ice won't melt.
>
> Rodents are part of its name.

The igneous rock is _____.

49

Take It For Granite

Granite is the most abundant of **intrusive rocks.** It consists of these minerals: quartz, feldspar, amphibole, and mica. Let's go on a granite hunt.

Use the clues to reveal where granite may be hiding out.

Clues

forms deep inside the earth	_ _ G _ _ _
surface of the earth	_ R _ _ _ _
the sides of a room	_ A _ _ _ _
roofed and walled structures	_ _ _ _ _ _ N _ _
larger than hills	_ _ _ _ _ _ I _ _
grave markers	_ _ _ _ _ T _ _ _ _
surfaces used to prepare food	_ _ _ _ _ E _ _

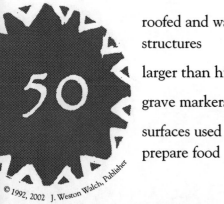

50

Extruders Appear

Extrusive rocks are igneous rocks formed when magma flows out over the earth's surface. Fast-cooling lava produces fine-grained rock.

Three fine-grained and two glassy-textured rocks appear in this puzzle. Use the Across/Down clues to help you find the answers.

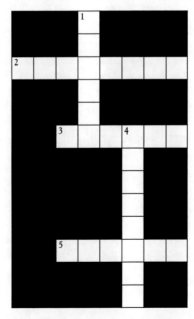

Across

   2. sounds like rhino light

   3. ba + NaCl

   5. pum + frozen water

Down

   1. sounds like Korea

   4. sounds like end in sight

51

Igneous Takeover

The earth produces a giant mass of intrusive **igneous rock.** What is it called?

To find out, supply the missing letters in the clues below. When you put the missing letters together, you'll know what the mass is called.

1. opposite of good: __ __ d.

2. Big Bang __ __ eory.

3. ring-shaped island of coral: at __ __ l.

4. earth's outer shell: l __ __ __ osphere

_____

52

Settling Sediments

Use these picture clues to create your own definition of sediment. Then consult an earth science textbook to see how well you did.

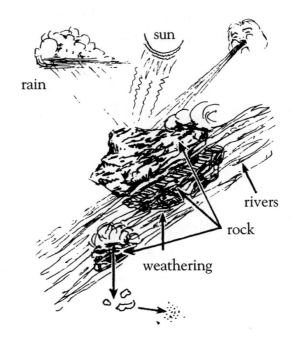

sun

rain

rivers

rock

weathering

My definition of sediment is

_____

_____

_____

_____

_____.

53

Sediment Roundup Puzzle

Natural forces and processes break down rocks, minerals, and organic matter into small particles. These tiny fragments are called **sediment.** Over time, the earth's forces and processes squeeze sediments together and turn them into sedimentary rock.

Try to solve the sediment puzzle. The idea is to collect SEDIMENT from the four terms below. Two adjoining letters in each term appear in the word SEDIMENT. Your job is to circle the adjoining letters in each term to produce SEDIMENT.

desert erosion

dirt

metamorphic rock

mountains

54

Mystery Sedimentary Rock 1

Sedimentary rocks form in layers from materials deposited by water, wind, ice, or other agents.

Combine nine of the letters in the boxes to uncover the mystery sedimentary rock.

Hint: It consists mostly of cemented grains of quartz sand.

d	g	e	o	t	e	l
e	i	a	e	u	s	y
a	n	r	l	n	i	m
s	o	a	i	h	c	o

55

Mystery Sedimentary Rock 2

Read the clues carefully. They will help you answer the question.

What sedimentary rock is a mixture of rounded pebbles of any shape or kind?

Clues

I'm a *con*, but I've never been arrested.

The middle of my name rhymes with *Tom*.

The last five letters of my name have a rodent between two *e's*.

_____

56

Mystery Sedimentary Rock 3

The clues will help you find the name of the mystery sedimentary rock, which is a smooth, soft, easily broken, impermeable rock.

Clue #1. "__ __. The baby's asleep."

Clue #2. a fermented malt with hops: __ __ __

Put these clues together and you'll get _____, a common sedimentary rock.

Here's another **hint:** The answer has five letters.

57

Sedimentary Rest Stop

Fossils are preserved evidence of past geologic life. Sedimentary rocks provide a good environment for fossil preservation.

In the series of letters below, find and circle the names of three sedimentary rocks known to contain plant and animal fossils.

slateporphyrybasaltsandstonecrystals

syenitemarbleshalegneissdoleriteiron

limestoneserpentinebiotitehornblende

58

Down Deep

Metamorphic rocks form only at great depth or at high temperature. Sedimentary rock and igneous rock can be transformed into metamorphic rock. For example, shale—slate and sandstone—quartzite.

What sedimentary rock transforms into marble? If you put the following clues together, you'll have the answer.

green citrus fruit   +   rocklike material

_____

Challenge: Come up with your own clues. Create a puzzle to show the transformation of quartzite or slate.

Join the Band

Metamorphic rocks are grouped by texture. **Texture** refers to the structure of a rock's surface. Metamorphic rocks, such as slates, phyllites, schists, and gneisses, are **foliated.** This means they are banded, or layered. Schist and gneiss show heavy banding; slate and phyllite show little banding.

Fill in the sketches below to show how you think banding might appear in the rock samples.

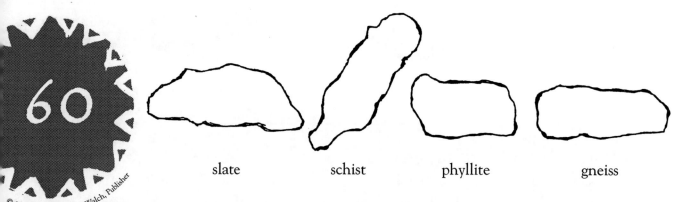

slate   schist   phyllite   gneiss

60

Growth Spurt

Crustal rocks warp, fold, and compress with heat and pressure. Heat and pressure cause physical and chemical changes in rock-forming minerals. The minerals may **recrystallize**—that is, they may melt and come out as crystals again.

Draw a series of sketches to show Rock A going through the recrystallization process.

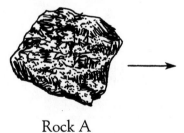

Rock A

61

Bumpy Road

Texture is the structure of a rock's surface. For example, slate, a metamorphosed fine-grained rock, has a smooth texture.

Are there rough- and coarse-textured metamorphosed rocks? Yes. In fact, the names of two of them can be found in the box below.

You'll need to put together different letters to spell the name of each rock. Write the name of each rock in the blanks under the box.

Hint: The name of the first rock sounds like *ice* or *rice*. The second sounds like *sports night*.

62

n	a	r	g	t
u	i	s	i	e
z	t	q	s	e

The metamorphosed rocks are __ __ __ __ __ __ and __ __ __ __ __ __ __ __ __ __.

Mystery Metamorphic Rock 1

Use the five clues below to help you identify the mystery metamorphic rock.

Clues

1. Most show a distinct banded structure.
2. Usually light colored
3. Commonest metamorphic rock
4. A coarse-textured rock
5. It looks something like this:

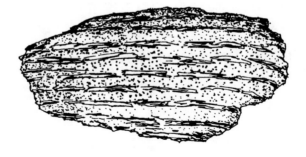

The mystery metamorphic rock is _ _ _ _ _ _.

Mystery Metamorphic Rock 2

Together, the 15 letters in the box form the name of the mystery metamorphic rock *and* the original sedimentary rock from which it came. Identify both the original sedimentary rock *and* the resulting mystery metamorphic rock. Use each letter only once.

o	e	m	r
e	i	■	n
a	b	l	e
l	t	m	s

The original sedimentary rock is __ __ __ __ __ __ __ __ __.

The mystery metamorphic rock is __ __ __ __ __ __.

64

Mystery Metamorphic Rock 3

These six words will help you identify the mystery metamorphic rock.

1. hard

2. massive

3. sandstone

4. durable

5. quartz

6. resistant

Bonus Clue: It's a wonderful *zite* to see.

The mystery rock is _____.

65

Find the Metal

What do elements that lose electrons easily and form positive ions have in common? They are all **metals.** Three examples are gold, silver, and zinc.

Arrange the clues scattered in the letters below, and you'll discover four additional metals.

Hint: Two of the metals are represented by their chemical symbols.

66

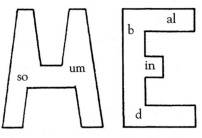

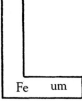

so um b al in d P um i Fe um

Metals in Hiding

Because their atoms are packed more closely together, **metals** are more dense than nonmetals. Nine metals are hiding in the list of words below. Either their names or their chemical symbols are keeping a low profile.

Go through the list and circle the name of each chemical element or its symbol that you discover. Then write the name or chemical symbol in the space provided.

Hint: Use a periodic table of elements.

Group Leader   Crane Operator
Tincture of Iodine   Environment
Alice Baxter (find 2) Mr. Custer
Nickelodeon   Return to Nature

1. _____   6. _____

2. _____   7. _____

3. _____   8. _____

4. _____   9. _____

5. _____

67

Ready Ore Not

You are digging in a rocky area, and you find samples of five different ores (metal compounds).

Ore #1. hematite

Ore #2. malachite

Ore #3. azurite

Ore #4. bauxite

Ore #5. cuprite

A stranger happens by, looks at your specimens, and says, "Wow! Three of these samples are copper ore."

Which samples do you think the stranger is talking about?

The stranger is talking about samples _____, _____, and _____.

68

Testing Your Metal 1

Match the metal in the left column with its description in the right column. Write the letter of the description next to the metal.

Metal

____ 1. copper

____ 2. lead

____ 3. magnesium

____ 4. aluminum

____ 5. tin

Description

a. silvery, lightweight

b. reddish metal; good conductor of electricity

c. silvery, soft metal; obtained from cassiterite

d. silvery, dense metal; extracted from galena

e. light, tough, silver-white metal

69

Nonmetal Hunt

Unlike metals, **nonmetals** have a dull luster. Nonmetals cannot be twisted, bent, or pounded without breaking. And nonmetals are poor conductors of heat and electricity.

Circle the names of five nonmetals hidden in the word lists below. Part of each name is in the First Word list; the rest of the name appears in the Second Word list. Circle each part and write the complete name in the space provided.

70

First Word	Second Word	Complete Name
1. escargot	1. bonded	1. _____
2. sparse	2. panic	2. _____
3. silt	3. iconoscope	3. _____
4. sulking	4. furrow	4. _____
5. harbor	5. noon	5. _____

Gem-boree

Beautiful, rare, and durable nonmetallic minerals are known as **gemstones.**

Use the clues to fill in the blanks and spell the names of five gemstones.

Clues	Gemstone
sounds like darn it	1. g __ __ __ e __
green gleam	2. __ m e __ __ __ __ __
pure C	3. __ __ __ __ o n __
sounds like *inspire*	4. s __ __ __ __ __ __ __
sounds like *so as*	5. t __ __ __ __

71

More Nonmetallic Minerals

The four **nonmetallic minerals** listed below help make life easier. Circle the mineral's name, its chemical symbol, or its chemical formula, and match the mineral with its use.

Nonmetallic Mineral

halite, salt, NaCl, CaCl, MgO

gypsum, sand, SiO_2, $CaSO_4.2H_2O$

SiO_2, bauxite, feldspar, Au, CO_2

NaCl, sulfur, carnotite, CaF_2, S

Use

food seasoning

plaster of Paris, plasterboard

make glass

gunpowder, medicines

72

Locating Nonmetal X

Write the underlined letter in each box below. Use the word clues next to the boxes to help you find the letters.

When you've correctly identified each one, unscramble the letters to find the name of Nonmetal X. Every clue describes the mystery nonmetal.

☐ <u>t</u>hin plates; known as soaps<u>t</u>one

☐ <u>c</u>rystals almost unknown; <u>c</u>olor—gray, white, or green

☐ si<u>l</u>icate of magnesium; basa<u>l</u> <u>c</u>leavage

☐ abund<u>a</u>nt mineral; <u>a</u>cids will not react with it

Answer __ __ __ __

73

Industrious Start

A **metalloid** has some of the properties of a metal and some of the properties of a nonmetal.

A metalloid important to industry is hidden in the puzzle below. Shade in the letters that spell its name.

Hint: Pure crystals of this metalloid are used as semi-conductors.

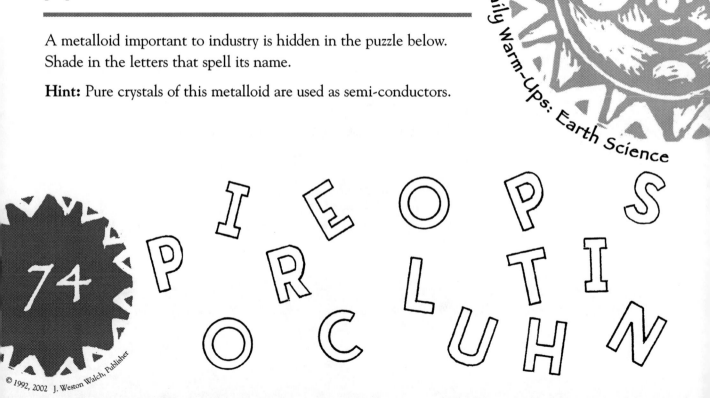

74

O₂ Origin

Some scientists believe the earth's original atmosphere came from a mixture of volcanic gases. The early atmosphere was very likely made of methane and ammonia, water, and carbon dioxide. Sunlight in the upper atmosphere caused water molecules to weaken, break apart, and free up oxygen.

Use the clues to identify mammals that need oxygen to survive on Earth.

Clues

rodent with small ears	__ O __ __ __
short-tailed carnivore	__ __ __ X
dog-like animal	__ __ Y __ __ __
car named after it	__ __ G __ __ __
weasellike, aquatic	__ __ __ E __
sirenian, sea cow	__ __ N __ __ __ __

75

© 1992, 2002 J. Weston Walch, Publisher

Breathe in, Breathe out

Plants and some other organisms release oxygen to the atmosphere through the process of **photosynthesis.** The oxygen they produce and the oxygen other organisms use remains in balance.

What percent oxygen is the earth's atmosphere?

The answer lies hidden in the box below. Read the letters left to right, starting with the top row. To find the answer, shade in only the *correctly spelled* numbers.

_____%

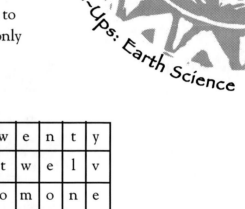

f	i	v	a	d	f	o	r	e	t	w	e	n	t	y
s	e	v	i	n	t	h	r	e	a	t	w	e	l	v
a	e	i	g	t	n	e	t	i	n	o	m	o	n	e

76

O Three

A small amount of oxygen can be found in the upper atmosphere. The oxygen there shields you from the sun's harmful ultraviolet rays. This oxygen molecule has three atoms of oxygen instead of the usual two, and it has a special name.

What is it? _____

Put the following hints together, and you'll have the answer.

Hint #1. The Wizard of   _____

Hint #2. 4, 3, 2, ?   _____

The name of the three-atom oxygen is

— — — — —

77

The Big N

Nitrogen makes up about 78 percent of the earth's atmosphere. Only three of the numbered statements about nitrogen, below, are true. If you add the numbers next to each of the true statements, you have the atomic number of nitrogen. But three *wrong* answers might also total the atomic number of nitrogen. How will you determine whether you have selected the three true statements about nitrogen?

I will determine whether the statements I selected are correct by

_____.

Statements

1. Nitrogen is needed by living organisms. (4)

2. Nitrogen is a noble gas. (2)

3. The atomic mass of nitrogen is 58.69. (3)

4. Most living things get nitrogen directly from the air. (2)

5. Nitrogen can be found in fertilizers. (2)

6. The chemical symbol for nitrogen is N. (1)

Plenty of Nitrogen 1

The **nitrogen cycle** supplies the atmosphere with nitrogen. Nitrogen enters the soil from the air. Then it goes into plants and then to animals before returning to the air. Plants need the help of certain microscopic organisms to change nitrogen from the air into nitrogen compounds in the soil.

Use the three clues below to learn what scientists call these microscopic organisms.

Clue #1. prefix designating nitrogen compounds: __ __ __ __ __

Clue #2. suffix meaning something that produces: __ __ __

Clue #3. word that means *repair:* __ __ __

The microscopic organisms are known as

__ __ __ __ __ __ __ __ - __ __ __ ing bacteria.

(1   )(2   ) (3   )

79

Plenty of Nitrogen 2

Nitrogen compounds enter an animal's body when it eats a plant. Nitrogen compounds return to the soil through animal droppings and rotting carcasses. What processes in the soil allow nitrogen to be released back into the atmosphere?

Decode the letter/word puzzle to reveal the answer.

d + night + tri + fee + k + shun

___ ___ ___ ___ ___ ___ ___ ___ ___ ___ ___ ___ ___ ___ ___ ___ ___ processes

80

Don't Forget CO₂

Carbon dioxide is a heavy, colorless gas. It makes up about 0.03 percent of the earth's atmosphere.

Are you ready for a challenge? See how many carbon dioxide molecules you can make from the elements in the box. You may use each element only once.

```
  C   O   O   C   C   O   O   O   C
O   C   O   O   C   C   C   C
      C   O   O   C   O   O   C   O   C   O
  C   O   C   O   O   O   O   O   C
```

81

Troposphere and Above

The **atmosphere** has five recognized layers. Label each layer in order by filling in the blanks with the missing letters.

___ ___ ___ sphere

___ ___ ___ ___ ___ ___ ___ sphere

___ ___ ___ ___ ___ sphere

___ ___ ___ ___ ___ ___ sphere

___ ___ ___ ___ ___ sphere

earth's crust

82

Plenty of Pressure

Use the clues in parentheses to fill in the missing letters. Then write each missing letter in order to reveal the mystery word. The mystery word names the instrument invented by Torricelli in 1643.

or__it (path)   tim__ (measurement)

o__sis (water)   neu__ron (nucleus)

sta__ (sun)   ign__ous (molten)

kil__ (prefix)   th__ust (force)

ato__ (smallest)

The instrument is a __ __ __ __ __ __ __ __ __.

This instrument measures _____ _____. (2 words)

83

Heat Energy

Heat energy can move in three ways.

1. Radiation, heat transfer in the form of electromagnetic waves

2. Convection, heat transfer in a liquid or gas caused by the difference in density and the action of gravity

3. Conduction, heat transfer through a solid, as one molecule collides with the next

For EACH of the three forms of heat energy, circle two related words in the puzzle. You may find the answers by reading up, down, forward, backward, or diagonally. Write your answers in the spaces beside the puzzle.

i	t	f	n	o	o	m
m	r	i	a	j	c	a
a	c	o	p	p	e	r
f	h	e	n	u	l	e
o	i	u	g	d	e	t
c	s	r	p	k	r	a
w	s	a	e	p	y	w

RADIATION _____ and _____

CONVECTION _____ and _____

CONDUCTION _____ and _____

Puzzle in the Air

The jumble of words below makes no sense. But if you put the words in order, they reveal something about the atmosphere and its relationship to the earth. Write the message—a compound sentence—in the space provided.

in changed earth's has changes atmosphere life affect conditions Life and the for atmosphere

_____

_____.

85

Bring on the Weather

Weather is what we call the day-to-day changes in wind, temperature, humidity, and air pressure.

In the puzzle below, empty spaces follow some of the letters in the word WEATHER. Fill in the spaces with weather-related words that start with that letter.

W. wind, water

E. _____ and _____

A. _____ and _____

T. temperature and _____

H. humidity and _____

E. _____ and _____

R. _____ and _____

86

Weather Tools 1

A **meteorologist** studies the weather and makes predictions based on measurements of temperature, air pressure, winds, and humidity.

Pretend you're a meteorologist who must predict tomorrow's weather. Fill in the missing letters in the names of the instruments you'll need to measure temperature, air pressure, wind, rainfall, and humidity. Tell what the instrument measures in the "What It Measures" column.

Instrument	What It Measures
r ___ in ___ a ___ ge (2 words)	_____
h ___ g ___ o ___ ___ ter	_____
an ___ m ___ meter	_____
___ he ___ m ___ ___ ete ___	_____
___ aro ___ ___ te ___	_____

87

Weather Tools 2

Read the three questions below. Then find the answer to each in the box below. Unscramble the circled letters in each correct answer to reveal the word that completes the mystery statement.

1. What instrument measures air pressure? _____

2. What instrument records air pressure? _____

3. What instrument measures altitude? _____

88

p(s)y c h o m e t(e)r	a(n)e m o m e t e(r)
a(l)t(i)m e t e r	b a r o g r a p(h)
b(a)r o m e t e r	s e i s m o g r(a)p h

Mystery Statement: __ __ __ __ forms when raindrops freeze into ice pellets.

Clouds Up Above

When air is cooled below its **dew point,** water vapor becomes liquid water. Condensation occurs, and clouds may appear. A cloud's shape depends on the air moving around it.

Circle the two words next to each basic cloud type that best describe it.

1. cumulus   puffy   icy   thin   cauliflower   heavy

2. stratus   low   billowy   feathery   layers   spiky

3. nimbus   dry   rain   wispy   snow   windy   flowery

4. cirrus   ice   low   drizzle   high   desert   misty

89

It's a Breeze

The sun is the major force that powers wind. **Wind** is air moving horizontally, parallel to the surface of the earth. Movement begins as warm air meets cool air. Moving air sets the major wind patterns in motion.

Put the scrambled, broken letters in order, and you'll identify four obstacles that reduce wind speed.

1. es + or + ts + f   _ _ _ _ _ _ _

2. u + il + ngs + di + b   _ _ _ _ _ _ _ _ _

3. ls + i + h + l   _ _ _ _ _

4. ta + mo + ns + i + un   _ _ _ _ _ _ _ _ _

90

What Goes Where?

Match each of the six weather symbols in the right-hand column with its meaning in the left-hand column.

Write the letter of the symbol next to the meaning.

___ 1. cold front   a.

___ 2. cloud coverage

___ 3. wind speed

___ 4. warm front

___ 5. wind direction

___ 6. snow

© 1992, 2002 J. Weston Walch, Publisher

Consider the Climate

Climate is long-term, widespread weather. There are three true statements about climate in the list below. Place an X next to the number of each true statement.

___ 1. Temperature and rainfall are main features of climate.

___ 2. Topography plays only a small role in climate control.

___ 3. Ocean currents are not a factor in climate control.

___ 4. Marine climates are relatively constant.

___ 5. Climate has no effect on weathering.

___ 6. A major influence on a region's climate is its latitude (distance from the equator).

92

What About Climate?

Climate is long-term, widespread weather, the average weather conditions over several years.

Circle the names of the three types of climates hidden in the puzzle. You may find the answers by reading up, down, backward, or diagonally.

```
z   a   p   d   n   i   w   d   k
o   e   o   p   a   e   r   a   w
n   c   l   s   g   y   a   b   a
e   t   a   r   e   p   m   e   t
a   j   r   a   i   n   f   a   e
l   e   e   w   a   r   d   i   r
y   t   i   d   i   m   u   h   i
```

93

Weather and Climate Riddles

Here are some riddles for you to solve. Be a creative thinker and let your imagination help you find the answers.

1. What kind of bean is part of the world climate?

   _____

2. What is something you do at lunch in all weather?

   _____

3. What does a t m o$_2$ s p h e r e represent?

   _____

4. What does this diagram tell you about Heather? $\dfrac{\text{the weather}}{\text{Heather}}$

   _____

94

Saline Along

Salinity is a measure of dissolved salt in ocean water or seawater. The average salinity of ocean water is about 3.5 percent. In some areas of the world, salinity may reach 4 percent or higher. What natural process might lead to higher salinity?

The underlined letters in the sentence below hold the answer. Place the letters in the proper order in the empty spaces to find the answer.

Its im<u>p</u>o<u>r</u>t<u>a</u>nt to <u>t</u>h<u>i</u>nk <u>a</u>bout th<u>e</u> <u>v</u>ery h<u>o</u>t su<u>n</u>.

_ _ _ _ _ _ _ _ _ _ _

A Salty Solution

Shade in the four terms listed below as they appear in the puzzle.
Your shading will reveal the chemical symbol for one of the
elements that make seawater salty. Some letters are used in more
than one word.

Terms

ice

net

sea

sun

g	l	a	c	i	e	r	a	o
u	s	e	a	o	i	n	u	a
y	u	i	e	s	c	o	r	e
o	n	e	t	i	e	o	n	u
t	t	u	n	a	m	i	s	a

The shaded portion reveals the chemical symbol Na __ __.

96

Keeping Current

The movement of ocean water in one direction is known as **current.** Winds produce surface currents.

Discover the three factors that determine the direction and flow of surface currents. Circle the letters that spell the missing word in each phrase below.

1. the (s a r e o l t i a p t e i m o s n) of the earth

2. landmass (e b t a r m e m r a i t e u r s) serve as obstacles

3. energy from the (o w e i t c n r d k) belts

97

© 1992, 2002 J. Weston Walch, Publisher

Wave Crave

Waves. High waves, low waves, freak waves—all kinds of waves. What three things create waves in the sea?

Unscramble each wave-shaped group of letters below to find the answer. Write the answers in the blanks.

 E T S D I
1.

 I S N D W
2.

T S A R Q H E K U A E
3.

_____   _____   _____

98

Exploring the Sea

Recent discoveries about the sea have been made using special equipment.

Find and circle the names of three items used to explore the ocean. You may find the answers by reading forward or backward.

```
        i t e s c l
        l
        l
        e
        t
        a
        s w r a n o s
                    p
                    s
                    e
                    n
                    i
        t v s u b m a r
```

What do your three answers have in common?

High Tech at Sea

Some high-tech operations use imaging equipment and software to make 3-D maps of objects on the seafloor, such as shipwrecks and aircraft debris.

Use the clues below to find the two-word name for the equipment that provides the images and data for software development.

First-word Clue: opposite of over + "two hydrogens and an oxygen"

Second-word Clue: s _ _ s _ _ s (Unscramble the missing letters: *n, r, o, e.*)

100

Sound on the Rebound

Scientists use **sonar** devices to determine the depth of the ocean. A transmitter bounces sound waves off the ocean floor and the waves return to a receiver.

Use the formula $D = \frac{1}{2} \times V$ to determine the depth of areas A, B, and C.

Note D = depth, $+t$ = elapsed time (sending/returning sound vibration), V = velocity (velocity of sound in water = 5,000 ft./second).

Area A $+t$ = 5.5 seconds

Area B $+t$ = 7.2 seconds

Area C $+t$ = 4.8 seconds

If Area B is one-mile long, what kind of undersea structure might A, B, and C represent? Circle the answer in the list below.

guyot   seamount

rise   canyon

plain   atoll

Down Deep

Underwater research vessels known as **submersibles** allow scientists to study the ocean depths. What are some of the things they examine?

Use the clues to help you fill in the blanks. The word MARINE refers to the sea.

Clues

solid material, at the bottom	_ _ _ _ M _ _ _ _
shrimps, crabs, etc.	_ _ _ _ A _ _ _ _ _
sunken ships	_ _ _ _ R _ _ _ _
aquatic vertebrates	_ I _ _
salt concentration	_ _ _ _ N _ _ _
deep furrows on the bottom	_ _ E _ _ _ _

102

Daily Warm-Ups: Earth Science

Seaward Terms 1

Unscramble the letters below to find the names of undersea structures. Then unscramble the underlined letters to discover the main food source for many ocean organisms.

1. s p n l a <u>i</u>

2. i d m - n <u>o</u> c e a   e r g i <u>d</u>

3. h <u>t</u> c r e n

4. t s n e <u>a</u> u o <u>m</u>

_____

103

© 1992, 2002 J. Weston Walch, Publisher

Seaward Terms 2

Use the clues to help you find four terms related to oceanography and write them in the puzzle below. You may write the answers either forward or backward.

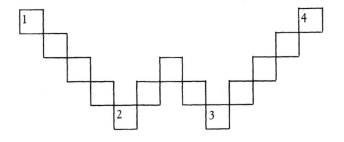

1. The part of the continent submerged beneath ocean waters

2. Earth's major energy source

3. Used to collect sea-life specimens

4. The daily rise and fall of ocean waters

Sea Floorshow

Find and circle five features of the ocean floor. The name of each begins with the letter *s*. Then write the words beside the puzzle. You may find the answers by reading up, down, forward, backward, or diagonally.

s	s	l	f	l	e	h	s
e	s	a	i	s	w	e	u
d	s	r	s	s	a	p	b
i	s	o	h	m	v	o	m
m	k	c	o	r	e	l	a
e	s	u	e	s	s	s	r
n	n	e	s	s	i	s	i
t	f	s	u	r	f	a	n
a	l	g	a	e	s	s	e

1. continental _ _ _ _ _ _

2. continental _ _ _ _ _ _

3. _ _ _ m _ _ _ _ _ canyon

4. _ e _ _ _ _ n _

5. _ e _ _ _ _ n _

105

Highs and Lows

The seafloor provides evidence of plate movement. Many scientists believe that heat energized by convection currents rises from the mantle. The heat flow elevates parts of the ocean bottom. What property of heat causes the land to rise?

Use the rhyming clues to tell you which letter to select. Then rearrange the letters to reveal the answer. The first example has been done for you.

1. score with four   s a p **a** n a p e   <u>a</u>

2. two will do   e s p e d a n d   __

3. pick six for kicks   s a n d a x e p   __

4. run with one   p a n a x e s d   __

5. survive with five   a n d p e d a p   __

6. no 11, try seven   s a n e s a d x   __

7. agree with three   s a n d s p a e   __

Answer: Heat __ __ **a** __ __ __.

106

Home of the Diatom

Use what you know or can find out about diatoms to complete the crossword puzzle.

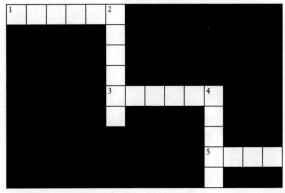

Across

1. Diatoms are not _____ or animals. Diatoms are algae.

3. They are one-_____ organisms.

5. They are an important _____ source for ocean life.

Down

2. Their shells are made of this material: _____. (Part of the word sounds "silly.")

4. They _____ about, wherever the sea carries them.

107

The Bottom Dwellers

Organisms that live on the ocean bottom are known as **benthos organisms.**

Combine any group of letters from the list below to name eight bottom-dwelling organisms. Use each group of letters only once.

cl	ish	rf
wo	ane	rm
mone	cr	spo
ab	ail	co
nge	ral	sn
sta	am	

1. _____   3. _____   5. _____   7. _____

2. _____   4. _____   6. _____   8. _____

108

Free in the Sea

Nekton, or free-swimming organisms, inhabit the sea in large numbers. They range in size from the tiny anchovy to the enormous whale shark.

Write the name of a free-swimming organism that begins with each letter of the word NEKTON.

N _____

E _____

K _____

T _____

O _____

N _____

109

Reef Grief

How much do you know about **coral reefs**? Circle the letters of the three true statements below about coral reefs.

a. Only part of a coral reef is made of living coral.

b. Water temperature must be between 20°C and 26°C to keep coral alive.

c. Corals are nekton organisms.

d. Coral animals produce calcite structures.

e. Corals grow best in deep water.

Use the circled letters to create a word that describes the relationship between a coral reef and a large ship. __ __ __.

Coral Pals

Look at the string of 46 letters below. Six organisms that live on or near a coral reef are hidden there. As you find each name, list it in the space provided. You may use the same letter twice for two different organisms.

polyplantseacucumbersandfeedsharkseelsandcrabs

1. _____

2. _____

3. _____

4. _____

5. _____

6. _____

Bad Weathering

Landforms are the result of both constructive and destructive forces. **Weathering** and erosion are destructive forces. For example, some metals deteriorate as a result of chemical weathering known as

— — — — — — — — —.

Use the clue below to find the answer hidden in the silly statement.

Clue: The silly statement is the worst. Pick the letters that are first.

Silly Statement: Candy or raisin raspberry okra sounds . . . icky, oozy, nasty.

Daily Warm-Ups: Earth Science

112

© 1992, 2002 J. Weston Walch, Publisher

Nothing Stays the Same

Chemical weathering causes some rocks to break apart. The action of rainwater, carbon dioxide, and oxygen may cause chemical weathering. Certain pollutants increase carbonic acid and sulfuric acid in the atmosphere. The result is acid rain.

Use the symbols in the box below to write the chemical formula for sulfuric acid five times. How many times can you write the chemical formula for carbonic acid with the symbols? To help you find the answer, here are the chemical formulas for each acid:

Sulfuric Acid H_2SO_4 **Carbonic Acid** H_2CO_3

```
S  O  H  O  S  O  H  H  O  O  H  H  C
O  H  H  O  O  H  S  O  O  H  C  O  O
H  O  O  C  S  O  H  C  H  H  O  C  H
H  C  H  C  H  O  O  O  S  O  O  S
O  O  S  H  O  S  H  C  O  H  H  O  H
O  S  H  O  H  O  O  H  S  O  C  H  O
```

Answer: _____

113

Hunka Ice

Glaciers are large bodies of slow-moving snow and ice that carry heavy loads of sediment. Glaciers collect boulders, gravel, and sand as they move. A glacier packed with debris becomes a powerful erosional agent.

Make a word out of six letters in the puzzle below that reveals what gives a glacier the power to erode the land. **Hint:** The glacier wouldn't have this power if it weren't for gravity.

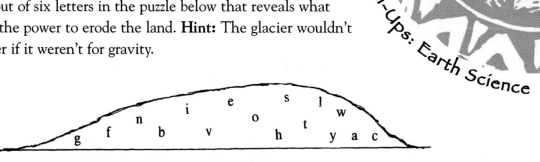

The word is __ __ __ __ __ __.

114

 115

Frosty Puzzle

A **glacier** may be described as a large mass of moving ice. Look at the word GLACIER. Did you know that you can use the letters in GLACIER to spell two of the words that describe it?

Find the two words and write them in the spaces below. You may use a letter more than once.

1. ___ ___ ___
2. ___ ___ ___ ___ ___

The Best of Weathering

Some of the results of **weathering** appear as letters, numbers, phrases, and symbols below.

1. *First Word* **or** (spelled backwards) + **ck**

   Second Word **f** + symbol for radium + **g** + opposite of women + **ts**

   ＿ ＿ ＿ ＿   ＿ ＿ ＿ ＿ ＿ ＿ ＿ ＿

2. bovine animal + unconscious part of the psyche + first letter in alphabet + four letters together that sound like *shun*

   ＿ ＿ ＿ ＿ ＿ ＿ ＿ ＿ ＿

3. r + the objective case of the pronoun we + t

   ＿ ＿ ＿ ＿

Erosion Explosion Puzzle

Erosion occurs when forces such as wind, water, and glaciers wear down the earth's surface.

Name two things that erode, transport sediment, change course, and flood their banks in natural and recurring patterns. Write your answers in the puzzle spaces. Then, accept a fun challenge. Write one answer upside down and the other backwards.

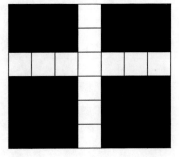

Water on the Go

Running water does a super job of eroding soil. Which features of the earth are eroded by running water?

To find out, fill in the blanks with the missing letters to form the words that provide the answers.

```
    p
    a  i                    c
       s                    r
    e     s     l           s              t
    a           o           s              e
R  U  N  N  I  N  G     W  A  T  E  R
o  s  d  d     d  r     h  t
      s           a     a           i  a
k     t                       l     m  c
                  i     f  l        e  e
      n           t     s  s           s
      e                          t
```

It's a Breeze

High winds can blow away fertile topsoil. In the United States, **wind erosion** destroyed much of the Great Plains during the 1930s.

The tragic event had a name. If you study the message below, you might discover the answer.

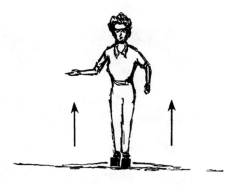

Donna Unger stood tall . . . but only with lifts.

The tragic event was called the __ __ __ __ __ __ __ __ __.

Something's Missing

Define each word in the hint list below to come up with six terms related to **erosion.** Letters appear in the puzzle to help you place the terms correctly.

Hint List

H_2O
Air in motion
Moving surface water
Slow-moving ice mass
To weather away
Force that pulls objects to Earth

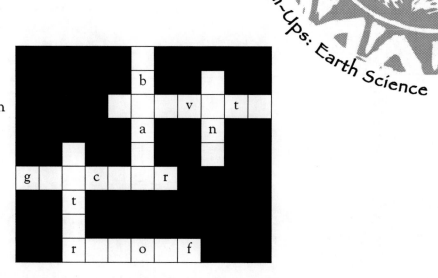

Down Under

Water hitting a level surface made of absorbent sediment sinks into the ground. Where does most of this **underground water** come from?

Look carefully at the diagram. It shows sedimentary rock with cracks that permit water to pass through. The source of most underground water is hidden in the diagram. See if you can shade in the answer.

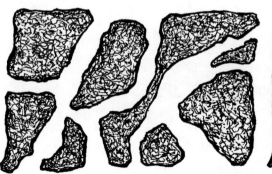

121

Aquifer Stir

An **artesian well** is a natural source of surface water that comes from an **aquifer** above an impervious layer of rock. An aquifer, then, is a water-holding layer of rock, gravel, and sand.

The names of two water-holding rocks are hidden in the puzzle. Follow the clue to find the answer.

Clue: If you darken i, b, and p, then the answer you will see.

i	c	o	p	n	g	b	l	i	o	m	p	e	r	b	a	t	e
b	p	b	b	i	i	a	i	b	n	i	i	d	p	i	i	b	i
s	b	a	i	n	p	d	s	p	b	t	b	o	n	b	e	i	p

_____ and _____

122

Stop and Go

Porous rock has open spaces, or pores, that allow the free flow of water. **Nonporous rock** has many tightly packed particles. Water cannot move quickly through nonporous rock.

In the space below, draw a picture of a porous rock, using circles to draw the pores. Draw arrows to show water flowing through the rock.

123

All Is Well

Water flows to the surface from the top of an **artesian well.** An **aquifer** is a porous layer above a nonporous layer. Pressure forces water from the aquifer up to the top of the artesian well.

Use the clues below to find out what water touches as it works its way to the top of the well. Fill in the missing letters in the puzzle.

Clues

bushes and flowers	_ _ A _ _ _
these anchor plants	R _ _ _ _
garden soil	_ _ _ T
tiny openings	_ _ _ E _
ants, for example	_ _ S _ _ _ _
well origin	_ _ _ I _ _ _
breaks or splits	_ _ A _ _ _
small rocks	_ _ _ N _ _

124

Hard Decision

Hard water contains the elements calcium, iron, and magnesium. Soft water is relatively free of minerals.

A grain is a unit of weight equal to 0.0648 g. Water that contains more than 8 grains of mineral matter per gallon is considered hard.

Circle the hard-water samples below.

Grains of Mineral	Gallons	Hard	
1. 1.037	2	yes	no
2. 0.3200	5	yes	no
3. 3.3200	8	yes	no
4. 0.2608	4	yes	no

125

Abrupt Erupt

Geysers are hot springs that erupt at regular intervals. Water becomes superheated underground, changes into steam, and explodes to the surface. The water evaporates, leaving behind mineral deposits.

The adjectives listed below describe these mineral deposits. The clue will help you unscramble the underlined letters to spell the name of the mineral deposits.

Clue: The name of the mineral deposits sounds like guy + sir + eye + tuh

126

beau<u>t</u>iful   mushroom-lik<u>e</u>

<u>s</u>oft   cauliflower-lik<u>e</u>

opaqu<u>e</u>   wh<u>i</u>te or g<u>ra</u><u>y</u>

po<u>r</u>ous

_ _ _ _ _ _ _ _ _

We Need the Water

Millions of people use **groundwater.** As the human population grows, more water is used, and the water table drops. A water shortage follows.

Use the letters in the word WATER to suggest water conservation methods. The first one is done for you.

Watch for leaky pipes and hoses. Repair them as needed.

A _____

T _____

E _____

R _____

127

Water Art

Water containing calcite drips from the roof of a cave and forms **stalactites.** Drippings from stalactites hit the cave floor to form **stalagmites.**

Use the number clues to put the correct letters in the puzzle. After you finish, take a good look. What problem do you see?

Number Clues

a. 3, 5, 14, 16

c. 17

e. 10, 21

g. 6

i. 8, 19

l. 4, 15

m. 7

s. 1, 11, 12, 22

t. 2, 9, 13, 18, 20

128

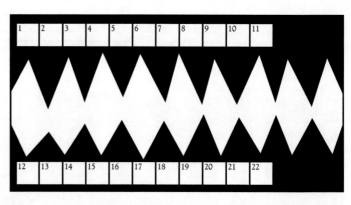

Water, Water

Water travels through **porous rock** (rock with openings, or pore spaces) until it reaches **nonporous** (tightly packed) **rock.** Since water can't penetrate the nonporous rock, it fills the pores at the bottom of the porous rock. As water continues to seep into the ground, the pore spaces fill with water until the porous layer becomes saturated, or thoroughly soaked. The water in the saturated portion is known as **groundwater.**

Make a diagram showing how groundwater forms. Use the following symbols on your diagram:

 – water

 – porous rock

 – nonporous rock

129

From Whence It Came

Put the letters listed below in their proper order. The clues that go with the letters will help you complete the task. What will you have when you're through?

Clues	Letters
Heavy ice pack forms.	E
New snow buries old snow.	C
Fresh snow falls.	L
Ice begins to move slowly.	R
Pressure builds.	I
Very cold area.	G
More snow falls.	A

The proper order of letters is as follows:

— — — — — — —

130

Daily Warm-Ups: Earth Science

Glacier Calling Card

Glaciers gather boulders, gravel, and sand. They become thicker and heavier and carve a trail as they move forward.

Glaciers leave marks and grooves on rock surfaces called

__ __ __ __ __ __ __ __ __ __.
1   2   3   4   5   6   7   8   9 10

To find the answer, use the clues below. Place your letter answers above the appropriate numbers.

Clues	Numbers
19th letter of the alphabet	1
prefix meaning *three*	2, 3, and 4
word meaning *in, near,* or *on a place*	5 and 6
electrically charged atoms	7, 8, 9, and 10

131

© 1992, 2002 J. Weston Walch, Publisher

Lighten the Load

Three kinds of deposits left by **glaciers** are hidden in the puzzle. In fact, they're very well hidden. One term is a compound word that is separated into two parts, and two terms appear backward. And there are two terms that do not apply.

See if you can find the answers.

Deposits: 1. _____

2. _____

3. _____ plains

```
e
n
o                               w
t                               a
s               s   r   e   k   s   e
d               n                   h
n               i
a       v   a   l
s               m
                o   u   t
                r
                d
```

© 1992, 2002 J. Weston Walch, Publisher

Glacier Retreat 1

Some people worry that as carbon dioxide increases in the atmosphere, trapped solar heat will create a global warming effect. **Global warming,** they say, will change the climate and may cause glaciers to melt, which would raise **sea level.**

List two problems a rise in sea level might cause.

1. _____

2. _____

133

Glacier Retreat 2

Some scientists believe a warmer climate might raise the melting rate of ice sheets known as **continental glaciers.**

Ice streams carry ice from inside glaciers to the sea. Scientists are concerned that fast-moving ice streams might cause a glacier to break apart.

Use the underlined numbers to find letters of the alphabet. Use these letters to fill in the blanks to name the high-tech equipment that is used to monitor ice streams.

First letter	15	16	17	<u>18</u>	19
Second letter	<u>1</u>	2	3	4	5
Third letter	<u>4</u>	5	6	7	8
Fourth letter	−3	−2	−1	0	<u>1</u>
Fifth letter	17	<u>18</u>	19	20	21

134

Scientists use high-tech equipment such as __ __ __ __ __ interferometry to monitor ice streams.

Continental Ice Machine

Continental glaciers are ice sheets that cover thousands of square kilometers of land.

Use the clues in the box below to discover the names of two landmasses covered by glaciers today. Write your answers in the space provided.

1. _ _ _ _ _ _ _ _ _ _ _ _

2. _ _ _ _ _ _ _ _ _ _

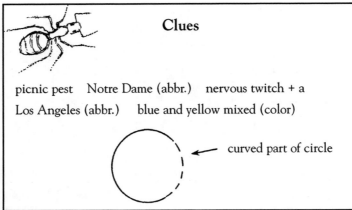

Clues

picnic pest   Notre Dame (abbr.)   nervous twitch + a

Los Angeles (abbr.)   blue and yellow mixed (color)

← curved part of circle

135

Four-Term Challenge

Four terms related to glaciers are hidden in the word-search puzzle below. You may find the answers by reading up, down, forward, backward, or diagonally. Use the clues to help you find the answers.

Clues

1. rhymes with *jerks* and *perks*
2. rhymes with *spill* and *hill*
3. sounds like *flames* and *brains*
4. sounds like *metals* and *petals*

136

```
n  s  i  r  s  k  r  u  l  s
a  s  e  l  t  t  e  k  c  e
m  f  t  u  o  d  a  n  s  t
e  i  t  e  q  m  l  b  k  t
s  l  e  f  e  r  l  k  r  l
a  l  r  s  m  h  i  a  o  e
f  r  a  m  e  s  t  c  w  s
```

r	o	c	h	e	a	f
o	r	e	k	s	e	i
c	a	i	r	t	s	r
k	e	t	t	l	e	n
	d	r	o	i	f	

Shape Up

A large, slow-moving **glacier** does a great job of eroding land. As a glacier moves down a valley, it grinds down and carries away practically anything in its path.

Use the clues below to identify three terms related to glaciers. You may find the answers by reading up, down, forward, backward, or diagonally. Shade in the letters to each answer in the puzzle. The shaded area will reveal the answer to the mystery question.

Clues

1. deepened valley with seawater

2. glacial hitchhiker

3. turns into compact ice

Mystery Question: What is the shape of a straight, smooth-sided glaciated valley?

It has a _____ shape.

137

Ice Age Rage

Many geologists believe an **ice age** is caused by three major events.

Select the groups of letters that belong together and, if necessary, unscramble them to find the missing word for each major event listed. Then write the word in the space provided.

tl	erut	era	it
pmet	ahs	ep	

1. a drop in _____ over time

2. changes in the _____ of the earth's axis

3. the _____ of the earth's orbit

Plate Fate

Plate tectonics theory explains that the lithosphere, the solid part of the earth, is made of enormous plates that move up, down, and sideways. This movement shapes the earth's crust. The major plates are named after continents they support.

Complete the puzzle below by writing the names of these continents.

```
__ __  r  __  P  __
            L
__ __ __  A  __ __  t  __ __ __
N  __ __  T  __    A  __ __ __ __  c  __
            E

__ __ __  T  __  a  __ __ __
            E
            C
            T
            O
       __  N  __  i  __
__ __ __  I  __  a
            C
            S  __ __ __ __    __  m  __ __ __ __ __
```

Awesome Force

According to **convection theory,** rocks in the mantle soften, expand, and rise. When they reach the base of the crust, they move horizontally, and cool. The cool material sinks. All this rising and sinking makes the crust bulge, buckle, and crack.

Unscramble the letters in parentheses, and write in the space provided what else you think the molten material might cause the crust to do.

_____ (tshecrt), _____ (nilerwk),

_____ (rpemcul), and _____ (arpw)

140

Spread the Word

Some scientists believe **convection currents** cause movement of the ocean floor away from either side of a mid-ocean ridge. Magma rising up from the mantle gives rise to a number of geologic events.

Circle four such events hidden in the box of letters.

m	i	n	e	r	a	l	e	a	r	t	h	q	u	a	k	e	s	r	o	c	k	s
g	e	y	s	e	r	s	h	o	t	s	p	r	i	n	g	s	w	e	e	l	l	s
g	l	a	c	i	e	r	s	v	o	l	c	a	n	o	e	s	f	a	o	r	d	s
c	r	y	s	t	a	l	s	s	t	a	l	a	c	t	i	t	e	s	i	r	o	n
m	e	a	n	d	e	r	i	n	g	s	t	r	e	a	m	s	f	l	o	o	d	s
d	i	n	o	s	a	u	r	f	o	s	s	i	l	s	c	l	i	m	a	t	e	i

141

Rattle and Roar

Most of the world's **earthquakes** and **volcanic eruptions** occur at **plate boundaries.** Plate movement produces stress, which in turn sets up conditions for volcanoes and earthquakes. The boundary of the plates underlying the Pacific Ocean is known as the Ring of Fire.

In the space next to each letter below, write a word associated with earthquakes or volcanoes that begins with the letter provided. The first one is done for you.

<u>Richter</u>   O _____   F _____
  I _____   F _____   I _____
  N _____   R _____
  G _____   E _____

142

Daily Warm-Ups: Earth Science

Under and Over

The earth is made up of **four layers.** The name of each layer lies hidden inside six of the 15 words listed below.

Write each name next to its description.

rustler	store	monetary
router	south	discard
albacore	syncline	thinner
dismantled	batholith	crustacean
Pangea	Atlanta	scoreless

Description

center of the earth; iron-nickel present

liquid iron-nickel present

zone of rock

thin, outermost layer

Name of Layer

_____ _____ (2 words)

_____ _____ (2 words)

_____

_____

143

Save Room for Dessert

The eight most abundant elements in the earth's crust are **oxygen, silicon, aluminum, calcium, iron, sodium, potassium,** and **magnesium.**

Find the chemical symbols for each of these elements hidden in the puzzle below. Some symbols appear more than once. Shade them in, and you'll discover the kind of dessert the earth provides.

S	O	F	t	N	w	M	N	a
i	j	e	T	a	E	g	Z	B
A	L	K	D	M	u	N	a	h
C	R	P	Y	g	H	O	x	d
a	U	b	j	F	T	K	y	W
O	w	G	r	e	p	O	C	a

144

Answer: crustal _____

A Volcano Is . . .

Use the words and the sketch to form a definition of a **volcano**.

(**Hint:** What's in the earth's crust?)

lava   hot rock   ashes   gases

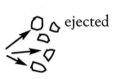 ejected

rock fragments

A volcano is _____

_____.

Erupting Words

You can easily find four common words in VOLCANO: *can*, *no*, *an*, and *a*.

Use letters from the word VOLCANO to form five more words that match the following definitions:

1. a fossil fuel   1. _ _ _ _
2. not excited; calm   2. _ _ _ _
3. social group based on   3. _ _ _ _
   common ancestry
4. fish-eating, diving bird   4. _ _ _ _ _
5. slang for crazy   5. _ _ _ _

146

Family de Lava

The scrambled words below represent six types of **lava.** Clues appear next to each scrambled word.

Unscramble the letters and write the correct answer in the space provided.

1. I D B N O A S I   Natural glass, sharp edges;   _____
shiny, curved, concave
surfaces

2. I L S E T E F   Fine-grained, light-colored   _____

3. A B L S A T   Fine-grained, dark-colored   _____

4. U E P C M I   Spongy appearance, may   _____
float on water

5. G O B A R B   Low-silica magma, dark-   _____
colored, coarse-grained

6. A D E S I A B   Coarse-textured, known   _____
as dolerite or trap rock

147

Volcanic Makeover

Crustal plate movement generates energy to produce **volcanic eruptions.** Volcanic eruptions build new landforms and, at the same time, change human and wildlife habitats.

List some of the effects of volcanic eruptions that can be harmful to humans and wildlife.

1._____

_____

_____

2._____

_____

_____

3._____

_____

_____

148

© 1992, 2002 J. Weston Walch, Publisher

Earthquake Alert

The plates that make up the earth's surface are in constant motion. **Earthquakes** often occur along the boundaries of crustal plates as plates move against one another or grind together.

Use the letters in EARTHQUAKES and PLATE TECTONICS to write the words you need to complete the puzzle below. You may use a letter more than once.

Down

1. strain

2. sharp, short sounds

Across

3. side-to-side motion

4. tremble

5. move back and forth quickly

149

Shear Delight

Write the term that fits next to its description. Then find the term in the puzzle and shade it in. You may find the answers by reading up, down, forward, backward, or diagonally. The shaded pattern will reveal which earthquake waves are known as **shear waves.**

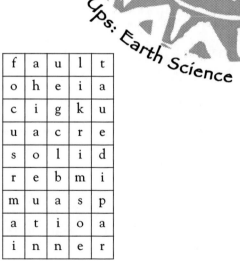

Descriptions

1. layer between the outer core and the center of the earth: _____ core

2. center of an earthquake: _____

3. states of matter: liquid, gas, and _____

4. a word meaning *fast* or *speedy:* _____

5. San Andreas is one: _____

f	a	u	l	t
o	h	e	i	a
c	i	g	k	u
u	a	c	r	e
s	o	l	i	d
r	e	b	m	i
m	u	a	s	p
a	t	i	o	a
i	n	n	e	r

Answer: _____ waves

150

Getting Together

Match the sketch on the right with the term on the left. Write the matching letter in the space.

_____ 1. *P* wave

_____ 2. epicenter

_____ 3. displacement

_____ 4. *S* wave

_____ 5. seismogram

a. wave →→ □

b. ᴡᴍᴡᴍᴡ‸ᴍ‸ᴍᴡᴡ

c. wave → liquid → wave →

d. ◁ ▷

e. [focus] point above focus
   focus

151

© 1992, 2002 J. Weston Walch, Publisher

Out of Position

The **Principle of Superposition** states that in undisturbed sediment, younger rocks are on top and older rocks are on the bottom.

Four different layers of rock are pictured out of order below. Number the layers from 1–oldest to 4–youngest, in the correct order.

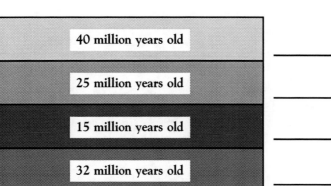

40 million years old	_____
25 million years old	_____
15 million years old	_____
32 million years old	_____

152

Keep it Active

Radioactive elements have an unstable nucleus that breaks down at a specific rate, a process called radioactive __ __ __ __ __. Scientists have figured out a way to use this process to measure the age of rocks. Evidence from geologic layers and radioactive dating indicates that Earth is approximately 4.6 billion years old and that life on this planet has existed for more than 3 billion years.

Combine three letters common to the words in column A with two letters common to the words in column B to find the missing word above—four times over!

A	B
decorate	okay
deck	Monday
decline	spray
decide	dismay

153

Guidelines

Scientists observe rock sequences and fossils to estimate geologic time. They use the known decay rates of radioactive isotopes to measure the time since the rock was formed. A **guide** or **index fossil** represents a typical organism from a particular time in geologic history.

Below are sketches of four guide fossils and their respective geologic times. Circle the correct name of each fossil.

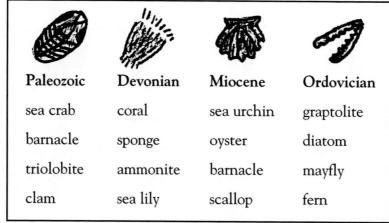

Paleozoic	Devonian	Miocene	Ordovician
sea crab	coral	sea urchin	graptolite
barnacle	sponge	oyster	diatom
triolobite	ammonite	barnacle	mayfly
clam	sea lily	scallop	fern

154

© 1992, 2002 J. Weston Walch, Publisher

Which Half?

Half-life is the time required for half the atoms in a radioactive substance to decay. For example, the half-life of uranium-238 is 4.5 billion years. That means it takes 4.5 billion years for half the atoms of a given mass of uranium-238 to decay to lead-206.

Use the letters in the box to make a list of six terms associated with **half-life.** You may use a letter more than once.

```
N E D Y U
A T I S M
R C O L B
```

The six terms are

1. _____

2. _____

3. _____

4. _____

5. _____

6. _____

155

© 1992, 2002 J. Weston Walch, Publisher

Carbon Copies

The **Cenozoic Era,** the Age of Mammals, has been going on for approximately 60 million years.

The terms listed below are sound-alikes for six different Cenozoic organisms. See if you can identify the organisms. Write the names in the space provided.

Sound-alikes

1. Newman, bloomin'   _ _ _ _ _

2. force, source   _ _ _ _ _

3. power, sour   _ _ _ _ _ _

4. funky, gunky   _ _ _ _ _ _

5. lass, mass   _ _ _ _ _

6. enamel, mammal   _ _ _ _ _

156

Early Going

The later era of **Precambrian** times is known as the **Proterozoic Era.** Volcanic action and extensive metamorphism of rocks occurred then. As you might suspect, no life existed on land. However, primitive invertebrates (animals with no backbone) lived in the seas.

Two primitive animal organisms thrived during this time. Do you know what they were?

The letters making up their names are scattered below. Use each letter once, put the animals back together, and list their names in the spaces provided. **Hint:** One animal name sounds like *term*; the other name rhymes with *lunge*.

Animal One:
_____

Animal Two:
_____

W   N   G

    S   R

O   M

    E   O   P

157

Age of Invertebrates

The **Paleozoic Era** lasted about 335 million years. During that time, invertebrates, fish, and amphibians developed.

Use the clues below to identify three common organisms that thrived during the Paleozoic Era. Write your answers in the space provided.

1.

   __ __ __ __ __ __

2. 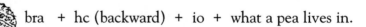 bra + hc (backward) + io + what a pea lives in.

   __ __ __ __ __ __ __ __ __

3. sun is one +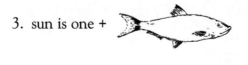

   __ __ __ __ __ __

158

Age of Reptiles

There were three distinct periods in the **Mesozoic Era: Triassic, Jurassic,** and **Cretaceous.** Reptiles thrived during one of these time spans. Which one was it?

The three scrambled clues below will provide the answer if you put them in the correct order.

Clues

1. It's melting! Keep what's left of the ice.

_____

2. A donkey is also known as an ___ ___ ___.

_____

3. The kind of cycle small children love to ride.

_____cycle

Unscrambled clues:

_____

159

Jurassic Classic

The **Jurassic Period,** or **Age of Dinosaurs,** lasted about 25 million years.

Five well-known dinosaurs lived during the Jurassic Period. Pieces of their names are scattered about within the sketch below.

See if you can put the names together.

1. _____
2. _____
3. _____
4. _____
5. _____

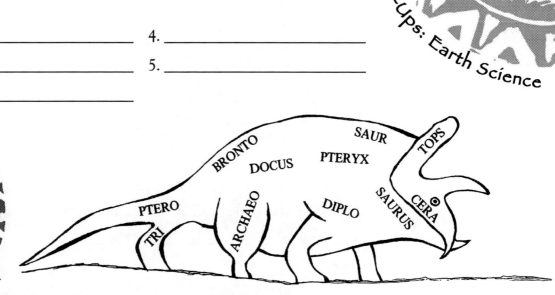

Mammal Roundup

The **Cenozoic Era,** the **Age of Mammals,** is approximately 60 million years old.

Numerous organisms—plant and animal—developed during this time. The terms listed below are sound-alikes for five different Cenozoic mammals.

Find a mammal for each of the paired sound-alike words. Write your answers in the spaces provided.

Sound-alikes

1. crewman, zoomin'   __ __ __ __ __

2. junk, trunk   __ __ __ __ __

3. force, source   __ __ __ __ __

4. frail, stale   __ __ __ __ __

5. spoon, lagoon   __ __ __ __ __ __

161

It Started With a Bang

The **big bang theory** places the origin of the universe between 10 and 20 billion years ago. According to the theory, the universe began in a ___Hot___ , ___dense___ state. The universe continues to ___expand___ .

Find and circle the three missing terms found in the puzzle below. Then write the terms in the space provided. You may find the answers by reading up, down, forward, backward, or diagonally.

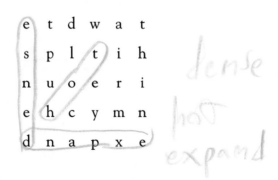

e	t	d	w	a	t
s	p	l	t	i	h
n	u	o	e	r	i
e	h	c	y	m	n
d	n	a	p	x	e

dense
hot
expand

162

Universal Appeal

The **universe** is a collection of everything that exists, the **cosmos.**

Use the letters in the box to supply the first two or last two letters of objects known to exist in the universe. You may use a letter more than once.

m d c r g a e s t o p l n

1. __ __ l a x i __ __
2. M e t e r o i d s
3. M e t e o r s
4. __ __ b u l __ __
5. __ __ v __ __

163

Too Hot to Handle

Of the following statements about the planet **Mercury,** four are true.
Connect the underlined letters in the correct items, and you'll
reveal the missing word in the statement below.

1. Mercury is the closest planet to the <u>s</u>un.

2. <u>M</u>ercury's diameter is approximately 7,700 miles.

3. Mercury has no known sa<u>t</u>ellite.

4. The length of a year <u>on</u> Mercury is about 225 days.

5. Mercury is about 60,000,000 miles <u>fr</u>om the sun.

6. Mercury is about as bright as <u>a</u> first-magnitude star.

7. <u>M</u>ercury is larger than Venus.

8. For the most part, Me<u>r</u>cury is difficult to see.

Mercury is seen only as an evening or a morning ___ ___ ___ ___.

164

Earth Twin

Venus, the second planet from the sun, is similar in size to Earth.

Let the hints about Venus on the left help you find the missing letters on the right.

Hints

lands between mountains	V _ _ _ _ _ _
surface rock	_ _ _ _ _ _ E
none present	_ _ _ N _
cloud content, acid	_ _ _ _ U _ _ _
surface rock	_ _ S _ _ _

165

Martian Zone

Scientists think **Mars,** the fourth planet from the sun, has a structure similar to Earth. Its four seasons and length of day are nearly identical to ours.

Use the clues to help you circle the letters on the right that match the descriptions. The uncircled letters, from left to right, will fill the blanks and complete the mystery statement below.

Clues

Olympus Mons is one.	1. cvoilctanto
molten rock	2. ltnakva
trapped in ice caps	3. hwatetr
Mars spacecraft	4. Viakirng
CO_2	5. caarbyon diaoxvide (2 words)
strong winds bearing clouds of dust	6. udunsnt wsetormrs (2 words)

Mystery Statement: S __ __ e n __ i s __ s __ h i __ __
t __ a __ M __ __ s m __ __ o n c e h __ __ e had
r __ n __ i __ g __ a t __ __ .

166

Mr. Big

Jupiter, the largest planet in the solar system, has a diameter of approximately 88,000 miles.

Use the clues about Jupiter to help you complete the puzzle.

Across

3. _____ atmosphere

5. orbit period, _____ years

6. no evidence of _____

Down

1. strong _____ field

2. a Jupiter moon

4. Great Red _____

Ring Thing

Saturn, the second largest planet in the solar system, has a density so low that it could float on water!

Use the clues about Saturn to help you fill in the spaces with letters that complete the terms related to the planet Saturn.

Clues

1. _____ in distance from the sun

2. this field is weak

3. similar to this planet

4. colorful bands

5. one of its gases

6. has at least twenty

Seventh Choice

Uranus, a gaseous planet, lies about 1.8 billion miles from the sun. It takes 30,660 Earth days for Uranus to make one revolution around the sun. Uranus is the seventh planet from the sun.

Use the clues under each box of letters to identify terms related to the planet Uranus. (Note: There are extra letters in each box.) Write each term in the space below the box.

1.

r	g	o
■	c	e

dense, rocky

2.

r	t	r	v
b	■	i	o

84 Earth years

3.

n	o	d	a	h
y	e	■	g	r

atmospheric gas

4.

e	h	m	e
n	a	t	y

atmospheric gas

5.

o	s	o
e	m	n

10 or more

6.

n	l	e	u	g
b	o	e	r	e

color of planet
(hyphenated word)

169

Far Out

Neptune, the eighth planet from the sun, is visible only through a telescope. Neptune, as you might imagine, has no water or air to sustain life. Therefore, life as we know it couldn't exist on Neptune.

Knowing this, complete the last line in the limerick. The last line should have no more than nine syllables.

There once was a planet Neptune,
Surrounded by more than one moon;
If you tried to live there,
With no food and no air,

_____.

Last in Line

Pluto, discovered in 1930, is about 3.7 billion miles away from the sun. Pluto is the ninth planet from the sun.

Use the clues about Pluto to identify the terms that fit the puzzle. You may find the answers by reading forward, backward, or upside down.

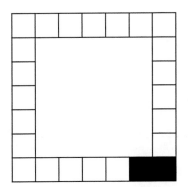

1. This is weak; it won't allow Pluto to hold its atmosphere.
2. The atmosphere during Pluto's summer is _____.
3. Only 0.18 times that of Earth's _____.
4. Orbit's sun in 248 Earth _____

171

Cosmic Belt

Let's find out how much you know about **asteroids,** orbiting space rocks. Supply the missing letters in the statements below.

1. Asteroids are chunks of rock known to exist between

   ___ a ___ s and Jupiter.

2. Asteroids o __ __ __ t the sun.

3. __ __ r e s is the largest known asteroid.

4. M __ __ e __ r i __ __ s are thought to be asteroid fragments.

5. Radar images show the existence of paired asteroids. They are called

   __ i __ a r __ asteroids.

172

Bright Delight

Comets are small, frozen masses of dust and gas that revolve around the sun. They are believed to be billions of years old.

Find the missing part of the incomplete words in the box and then write them in the spaces provided.

amm	zone	dy	car	lion
tric	ta	pla	ize	hyd
met	ates	rt	nuc	rac

1. Shape of a comet's orbit is eccen __ __ __ __.
2. A comet is a collection of icy rock containing __ __ __ onia and __ __ __ hane.
3. Scientists think a great sphere known as the Oo __ __ Cloud contains billions of comets.
4. A comet's point in orbit nearest the sun is known as perihe __ __ __ __.
5. As a comet nears the sun, parts of it vapor __ __ __.
6. The head of a comet includes the nucleus and coma. A comet's mass is in the __ __ __ leus.

173

Damp Discovery

Astronomers have recently reported finding water on **comets** orbiting a distant star. According to the report, the discovery may indicate the existence of planetary systems similar to our own, with the essential ingredients for life as we know it.

Find and circle eight terms related to WATER. You may find the answers by reading up, down, forward, backward, or diagonally.

```
o  s  d  u  o  l  c  w
x  r  m  k  n  i  r  d
y  t  a  x  k  q  c  b
g  b  p  i  v  u  t  e
e  f  i  l  n  i  v  t
n  e  g  o  r  d  y  h
```

174

Space Chips

A **meteor** is a rock particle that burns up in space. A **meteorite** is a rock particle that actually reaches the earth's surface.

Unscramble the four statements below describing a *meteorite*.
Hint: Each sentence begins with a capitalized word.

1. that been years old have Meteorites billion one-half and are four found.

2. tons weigh meteorites several Large.

3. iron meteorites of and nickel Some made are.

4. Large Canada found have Russia in meteorite Arizona craters been and.

Unscrambled Statements

1. _____

2. _____

3. _____

4. _____

175

© 1992, 2002 J. Weston Walc

Telescope 1

A **telescope** is an optical instrument used by astronomers to see distant objects.

To find out what can be seen through a telescope, fill in the blanks in the puzzle below with the missing letters.

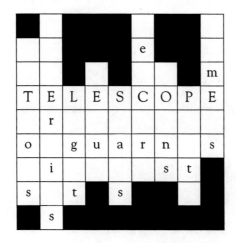

Telescope 2

The **Hubble space telescope** was launched in April 1990. The telescope carries a 95-inch mirror and numerous scientific instruments. Several hundred astronomers, computer scientists, and technicians control the orbiting telescope.

Unscramble the terms in parentheses to find out what scientists observed with the Hubble space telescope. Write your answers in the spaces provided.

1. The Hubble space telescope sent back detailed images of certain (e x a s g a i l) _____.

2. The Hubble space telescope was able to (s u e m e r a) _____ the (s o n t i o i p) _____ of stars.

3. The Hubble space telescope produced evidence for the existence of (k c l a b) _____ (s l e o h) _____.

4. The Hubble space telescope produced images of several (a p s n e l t) _____.

5. The Hubble space telescope photographed an array of (l c e a l s e t i) _____ bodies.

177

Festival of the Moons

Two things are certain about Earth's **moon:** It's smaller than planet Earth and it orbits the planet. How much do you know about other moons in our solar system?

To find out, take this Moon Quiz.

1. How many moons does Mercury have?

   a. 0   b. 1   c. 2   d. 3

2. How many moons does Venus have?

   a. 0   b. 1   c. 2   d. 3

3. Jupiter has at least

   a. 12 moons   b. 14 moons   c. 15 moons   d. 16 moons

4. This moon belongs to Saturn.

   a. Charon   b. Titania   c. Titan   d. Ariel

5. Uranus has at least

   a. 8 moons   b. 12 moons   c. 15 moons   d. 20 moons

178

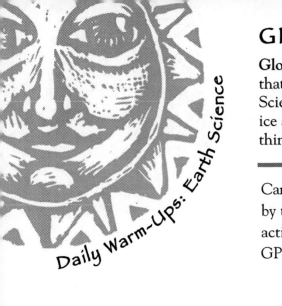

GPS

Global Positioning System (GPS) is a radio-navigation system that uses satellites to calculate positions anywhere on the earth. Scientists can use GPS to monitor the earth's surface, the size of ice sheets in Greenland, or volcanic activity, among many other things.

Can GPS be used for recreational activities? Yes, especially by those with an interest in technology. Find three recreational activities hidden in the puzzle below that might make use of GPS and circle them.

```
M D A N C I N G E L
H I V I K I H I K I N G O
B F I S H I N G E M O
F R E A D I N G R L P I N G
A R U N N I N G R A C I N G
E N A V I G A T I O N A L R A F T
W S U R F I N G A K C A N O E
C A L F R O P I N G
```

179

Stars and Galaxies

Use the scattered letters to spell the words that match the clues.
A letter may be used more than once.

180

Clues

Ursa Major	1. _ _ _ _ _ _ _ _ _
less luminous star	2. _ _ _ _ _ _
self-explosive star	3. _ _ _ _ _ _ _ _ _ _
huge cloud of gas and dust	4. _ _ _ _ _ _ _
a star's true brightness	5. _ _ _ _ _ _ _ _ _ _ _

1. Illustrations will vary.
2. 1. man + ax + i + an + der = Anaximander
   2. ot + le + rist + a = Aristotle
   3. pic + e + us + u + r = Epicurus
3. Oxygen
4. The word is lithosphere.
5. 1. b (inner core)   3. a (mantle)
   2. d (crust   4. c (outer core)
6. rock, core, dense, part, earth; crust—oil;
   mantle—iron; core—nickel
7. geologist
8. 1. volcano; 2. earthquake; 3. trilobite (fossil);
   4. water
9. 1. abyssal plain; 2. slope; 3. canyon or trench;
   4. volcanoes
10. 1. fault; 2. telescope; 3. stalactites; 4. geyser;
    5. crust
11. 1. earthquakes; 2. volcanic eruptions;
    3. mountain building
12. (animals) H—horse, hamster, hyena, heron
              M—moth, monkey, muskrat, mole
              S—snake, sloth, salamander, sheep

(plants) H—heather, hyacinth, horsetail, hedge
         M—mustard, moss, marigold, magnolia
         S—sunflower, spruce, sequoia, squash
13. Horizon A—humus, roots, sand
    Horizon B—clay, sand, silt
    Horizon C—weathered bedrock
14. 1. cartographer; 2. seismologist; 3. petrologist;
    4. paleontologist; 5. hydrologist; 6. geologist
15.
```
S A C J A L E
O E I U L S I
L A D P P M O
U D N I W A T
A E L I T R U
B C G E A S L
E V I R O A P
```
16. A = 3.2; B = 4.8; C = 1.7. Substance B has the
    highest specific gravity. The average specific gravi-
    ty is 3.2, the same as Substance A.
17. Jenny's object has a density of 3.19 g/cm^3.
    Margaret's object has a density of 2.86 g/cm^3.
    Jenny wins.

Daily Warm-Ups: Earth Science

18. 1. a speed skater making a quick turn
2. a fast-moving race car turning over and over
3. a person swinging a weight on a rope
4. a rollerskater rounding a curve
5. a whirling ballerina.
6. a spinning top
19. Globe, papeR, chAir, Vase, pencIl, Teacher, You
20. 1. ton, b   2. gram, a   3. kilogram, c
21. 1. Circle: As (arsenic) and Co (cobalt)
2. Circle: No (nobelium), Fr (francium), and I (iodine)
3. Circle: W (tungsten), Be (beryllium), Au (gold), and Ca (calcium)
4. Circle: Ar (argon), Mo (molybdenum), and Na (sodium)
5. Circle: V (vanadium) and S (sulfur)
22. 1. HNO_3 4. Al_2O_3
2. H_2SO_4 5. H_2O_2
3. FeS_2 6. $CuSO_4$
I noticed that five of the chemical compounds include the element oxygen.

23. Statements 2 and 4 correctly describe a proton. The shaded 2s and 4s in the puzzle reveal the symbol for potassium (K).

24. Statements 1, 3, and 5 correctly describe an electron. The shaded 1s, 3s, and 5s in the puzzle reveal the symbol for hydrogen (H).

Daily Warm-Ups: Earth Science

25. Statements 3 and 4 correctly describe neutrons. The shaded 3s and 4s in the puzzle reveal the symbol for carbon (C).

2	2				2	1
5	1	5	1	2	5	1
2	5	5	2	5	1	5
1	2	1	1	2	2	5
1	5				5	1

26. Accept any reasonable answer.
27. A chemical change occurs in examples 3 and 5.
28. 1. chair (solid)   4. steam
    2. kerosene   5. limewater
    3. carbon (solid)   6. rubber (solid)
29. The circled words are *steam*, *vapor*, *air*, *oxygen*, and *helium*. The uncircled words—*magnesium*, *copper*, *crystal*, and *sodium*—are examples of solids.
30. sauCe, blOod, Honey, watEr, Sweat, mIlk, Oil, raiN
31. Models will vary.
    Teaching Tips and Suggestions:
    Allow students to look in textbooks and elsewhere for examples of atomic models.
32. radioactive elements
33. Sketches will vary.
34. 1. amphibole   7. chlorite
    2. pyroxene   8. quartz
    3. feldspar   9. serpentine
    4. muscovite   10. talc
    5. biotite   11. stilbite
    6. olivine   12. analcite
35. 1. SiO_2 2. $ZrSiO_4$ 3. $MnSiO_3$
    4. $KAlSi_3O_8$
36. 1. galena 2. halite 3. calcite 4. quartz
    They are all solid, inorganic chemical substances found in the earth's crust.
37. Hardest—Mineral Y
38. Calcite
    Teaching Tips and Suggestions:
    Students will find the missing letters quickly. The real challenge comes in unscrambling the letters.
39. 1. glacier   4. geode
    2. cleavage   5. pluton
    3. geyser   6. mantle
    The mystery crystal is garnet.

Daily Warm-Ups: Earth Science

Answer Key

40. From top to bottom: mercury, gold, and galena (lead ore)
41. Mor<u>cuber</u>, <u>Nadine C</u>. <u>Leiter</u>, ba<u>salt</u>, <u>Crystal</u> <u>Lecuben</u>, and <u>Nadine</u>'s
42. 1. d; 2. f; 3. e; 4. a; 5. b; 6. c
43. The statement is true. Mineral X = 4.57 or 4.6; Mineral Y = 4.4
44. The combined first letters spell *minerals*, what the mountain is made of.
45. The earth's INTERNAL HEAT
46. Type 1. sedimentary: se + **dime** + n + **tar** + y
    se + U.S. coin = <u>dime</u> + n + solid particle in tobacco smoke = <u>tar</u> + y
    Type 2. igneous: ig + **neo** + **us**
    ig + three-letter prefix meaning <u>new</u> = <u>neo</u> + objective case of we = <u>us</u>
    Type 3. metamorphic: **meta** + m + **or** + phic
    prefix meaning change in form = <u>meta</u> + m + conjunction introducing the second of two possibilities in a series = <u>or</u> + phic
47. 1. granite   3 obsidian
    2. basalt   4. pumice
48. obsidian
49. Pumice. The ice in pumice is, of course, pum*ice*. Rodents as part of its name? Pu*mice*.
50. maGma, cRust, wAlls, buildiNgs, mountaIns, tombsTones, countErs
51. Across: 2. rhyolite   3. basalt   5. pumice
    Down: 1. scoria   4. andesite
52. batholith
53. Sediment is small particles of rock that have been broken down by physical and chemical means.
54. de<u>se</u>rt erosion (se), <u>di</u>rt (di), <u>me</u>tamorphic rock (me), mou<u>nt</u>ains (nt). The adjoining letters = se + di + me + nt = sediment.
55. sandstone
56. Conglomerate
57. Clue #1: Sh; Clue #2: ale
    Put them together and you get sh + ale, or *shale*.
58. First row: sandstone; second row: shale; third row: limestone
59. Limestone. Individual puzzles will differ.
60. slate—little banding; schist—heavy banding; phyllite—little banding; gneiss—heavy banding

61. Sketches will vary.
62. First rock: gneiss; second rock: quartzite
63. gneiss
64. original sedimentary rock: limestone
   mystery metamorphic rock: marble
65. quartzite
66. P + b = Pb (chemical symbol for lead)
   so + d + i + um (sodium)
   al + um + in + um = aluminum
   Fe (chemical symbol for iron)
67. NOTE: Make sure each student has access to a periodic table of the elements. Group Leader (lead); Tincture of Iodine (tin); Alice Baxter (Al - aluminum; Ba - barium); Nickelodeon (nickel); Crane Operator (Cr - chromium); Environment (iron); Mr. Custer (Cu - copper); Return to Nature (Na - sodium)
68. The stranger is talking about sample 2: malachite; sample 3: azurite; sample 5: cuprite.
69. 1. b   3. e   5. c
    2. d   4. a

70. 1. car + bon = carbon   4. sul + fur = sulfur
    2. arse + nic = arsenic   5. bor + on = boron
    3. sil + icon = silicon
71. 1. garnet   3. diamond   5. topaz
    2. emerald   4. sapphire
72. Food seasoning: halite, salt, NaCl; plaster of Paris, plasterboard: gypsum, $CaSo_4.2H_2O$; make glass: SiO2, sand; gunpowder, medicines: sulfur, S
73. Unscrambling the letters t, c, l, and a shows that Nonmetal X is *talc*.
74. silicon
75. mOuse, lynX, coYote, jaGuar, ottEr, maNatee
76. Top row: twenty; bottom row: one. Together they spell twenty-one.
77. Hint #1: Oz; Hint #2: 1 (one) = Oz + one, or Ozone.
78. Statements 1, 5, and 6 added together total 7. A student would know if the statements are correct by researching nitrogen in the appropriate texts.
79. The microscopic organisms are known as nitrogen-fixing bacteria.

80. denitrification processes
81. ten carbon dioxide molecules, with six carbons remaining
82. From the earth up: troposphere, stratosphere, mesosphere, thermosphere, and exosphere
83. barometer. A barometer measures [atmospheric] *air pressure.*
84. RADIATION fire and sun;
    CONVECTION water and air;
    CONDUCTION iron and copper.
85. Life has changed Earth's atmosphere, and changes in the atmosphere affect conditions for life.
86. W: wind, water; E: eye (hurricane), energy, electricity; A: air, atmosphere, altocumulus, anemometer; T: temperature, thermal, tornado, typhoon; H: humidity, hail, hurricane; E: easterlies, evaporation; R: rain, radiation, raindrop, radar
87. rain gauge—rainfall amount
    hygrometer—humidity
    anemometer—wind speed
    thermometer—temperatures
    barometer—pressure

88. barometer, barograph, altimeter
    The unscrambled letters spell *Hail.*
89. 1. cumulus—puffy, cauliflower
    2. stratus—low, layers
    3. nimbus—rain, snow
    4. cirrus—ice, high
90. 1. forests   3. hills
    2. buildings   4. mountains
91. 1. d   4. a
    2. f   5. b
    3. e   6. c
92. 1. true (X)   4. true (X)
    2. false   5. false
    3. false   6. true (X)
93. Temperate, polar, and dry

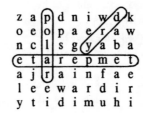

94. 1. lima (c<u>lima</u>te)
2. eat (w<u>eat</u>her)
3. oxygen in the atmosphere
4. It says that Heather is under the weather.
95. evaporation
96. The shaded portion reveals the chemical symbol for chlorine, Cl. Na (sodium) and Cl produce NaCl, sodium chloride, or salt.

g	l	a	c	i	e	r	a	o
u		o		n	u	a		
y		i	e	s		o	r	e
o			i		o	n	u	
t	t	u	n	a	m	i	s	a

97. 1. rotation   2. barriers   3. wind
98. 1. tides   2. winds   3. earthquakes
99. Satellites, sonar, and submarines. All three answers begin with the letter *s*.
100. First word: *underwater*. Second word: *sensors*.
101. Area A = 13,750 feet; Area B = 18,000 feet; Area C = 12,000 feet. The undersea structure would probably be a *canyon*.

102. Top to bottom: sediMents, crustAceans, shipwRecks, fIsh, saliNity, trEnches
103. 1. plains   3. trench
2. mid-ocean ridge   4. seamount
The *diatom* provides the main source of food.
104. 1. shelf   3. net
2. sun   4. tides
105. 1. shelf or slope   4. seamount or sediment
2. shelf or slope   5. seamount or sediment
3. submarine
106. Heat expands.
107. Across: 1. plants   3. celled   5. food
Down: 2. silica   4. drift
108. wo+rm, ane+mone, spo+nge, cr+ab, co+ral, sn+ail, sta+rf+ish, and cl+am
109. N—needlefish, nurse shark
E—eel, electric ray
K—kelp bass, kingfish, king salmon
T—tuna, tiger shark, tarpon
O—opaleye, ono, ocean perch
N—Nassau grouper, northern scup

Daily Warm-Ups: Earth Science

110. Statements a, b, and d are true. The relationship is *bad*.
111. 1. polyp   4. sharks
     2. plants   5. eels
     3. sea cucumbers   6. crabs
112. corrosion. The clue highlights the first letters in each word in the silly statement, which combine to spell "corrosion."
113. four times
114. weight
115. ice and large
116. 1. rock fragments
     2. oxidation
     3. rust
117. rivers and streams

118.

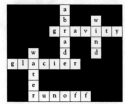

119. The first letter of each word in the message spells the name of the tragic event: *Dust Bowl*.
120. H_2O—water
     Air in motion—wind
     Moving surface water—runoff
     Slow-moving ice mass—glacier
     To weather away—abrade
     Force that pulls objects to Earth—gravity

121. rain
122. conglomerate and sandstone
123. Drawings will vary. The arrows should show water moving through porous layers and moving slowly or not at all in nonporous layers.
124. Top to bottom: plAnts, Roots, dirT, porEs, inSects, aquIfer, crAcks, stoNes
125. 1. no   3. no
     2. no   4. no
126. geyserite
127. A. Adjust sprinklers to minimize waste.
     T. Timing devices, especially for sprinklers, control overuse.
     E. Early-morning watering allows water to penetrate the soil.
     R. Rotate watering days. Water every other day, for example.
128. stalagmites (1–11) and stalactites (12–22)
     Problem: The stalagmites are forming on the roof of the cave, not on the floor, and the stalactites are on the floor, not on the roof.
129. Diagrams will vary.
130. The proper order of letters spells GLACIER. You'll have a brief description of how a glacier forms.
131. 1—s; 2, 3, and 4—tri; 5 and 6—at; 7, 8, 9, and 10—ions. All letters together form the word STRIATIONS.
132. eskers, drumlins, and outwash (compound, two-part word)
133. Some shorelines would disappear, which could change the local ecosystem. Water would flood beaches. Glacial meltwater would dilute ocean salinity and perhaps kill marine organisms.
134. The numbers represent the order of letters in the English alphabet: 18 = r, 1 = a, 4 = d, 1 = a, 18 = r. Therefore, r + a + d + a + r = radar.
135. picnic pest = ant
     curved part of circle = arc
     nervous twitch + a = tic + a
     all together = *Antarctica* (#1)
     blue and yellow mixed (color) = green
     Los Angeles (abbr.) = LA
     Notre Dame (abbr.) = ND
     All together = *Greenland* (#2)

Daily Warm-Ups: Earth Science

136. 1. cirques   2. till   3. kames   4. kettles
137. 1. deepened valley with seawater = fiord
      2. glacial hitchhiker = rock
      3. turns into compact ice = firn.
      The shaded-in letters produce a U shape.
      Mystery Question Answer: "U" shape
138. 1. pmet + era + erut = temperature
      2. it + tl = tilt
      3. ahs + ep = shape
139. From top to bottom: EuroPe, L, AntArctica,
      NorTh America, E; AusTralia, E, C, T, O, INdia,
      AfrIca, C, South America
140. stretch, wrinkle, crumple, and warp
141. Row one: earthquakes. Row two: geysers, hot
      springs. Row three: volcanoes
142. R—Richter, rattle, rupture
      I—igneous, intrusive
      N—noxious
      G—gas, granite
      O—odor, obsidian
      F—flow, fault

F—fire, fracture, fallout
I—intrusion, invasion
R—rumble, roar
E—eruption, explosion
143. 1. inner core (th<u>inner</u>, alba<u>core</u>, or s<u>core</u>less)
      2. outer core (<u>router</u>, alba<u>core</u>, or s<u>core</u>less)
      3. mantle (dis<u>mantled</u>)
      4. crust (<u>crust</u>acean)
144. crustal pie (chemical symbols O, Si, Al, Ca, Fe,
      Na, K, Mg) NOTE: Make sure each student has
      access to a periodic table of the elements.

145. Answers will vary. A possible response might be as
      follows: A volcano is a vent in the earth's crust
      through which lava (hot rock), rock fragments,
      gases, and ashes are ejected.

Daily Warm-Ups: Earth Science

146. 1. coal   4. loon
     2. cool   5. loco
     3. clan

147. 1. obsidian, 2. felsite, 3. basalt, 4. pumice,
     5. gabbro, and 6. diabase

148. Among the possible responses: Hot lava spills into
the sea; water temperature rises; marine organisms
die; tsunamis; hot ash and lava.; poisonous gases;
destructive mud-flows

149. Across: 3. roll   4. quake   5. shake
     Down: 1. stress   2. rattle

150. 1. inner   4. rapid
     2. focus   5. fault
     3. solid
     Puzzle answer: *S* waves

151. 1. c   3. d   5. b
     2. e   4. a

152. Top layer 15 million years old
Second layer 25 million years old
Third layer 32 million years old
Fourth layer 40 million years old

153. Column A—first three letters are *dec*
Column B—last two letters are *ay*
dec + ay = decay

154. From top to bottom: trilobite, sponge, scallop, and
graptolite

155. time, uranium, years, mass, decay, and billion

156. 1. human   4. monkey
     2. horse   5. grass
     3. flower   6. camel

157. worm and sponge

158. 1. insect   2. brachiopod   3. starfish

159. 1. ic   2. ass   3. tri
The unscrambled clues spell *Triassic.*

160. BRONTOSAURUS, TRICERATOPS,
PTEROSAUR, DIPLODOCUS, and
ARCHAEOPTERYX

161. 1. human   4. whale
     2. skunk   5. raccoon
     3. horse
162. hot, dense state. . . . continues to expand

```
e t d w a t
s p l t i h
n u o e r i
e h c y m n
d n a p x e
```

163. 1. galaxies   4. nebulae or nebulas
     2. asteroids   5. novae or novas
     3. meteors
164. Statements 1 (s), 3 (t), 6 (a), and 8 (r) are true.
Mercury is the evening or morning *star*.
165. From top to bottom: Valleys, granitE, mooNs,
sulfUric, baSalt
166. 1. volcano   4. Viking
     2. lava   5. carbon dioxide
     3. water   6. dust storms
Mystery Statement: Scientists think that Mars
may once have had running water.

167. Across: 3. gaseous   5. twelve   6. life
Down: 1. magnetic   2. Io   4. spot
168. 1. sixth   4. clouds
     2. magnetic   5. hydrogen
     3. Jupiter   6. moons
169. 1. core   4. methane
     2. orbit   5. moons
     3. hydrogen   6. blue-green
170. Answers will vary.
171. 1. gravity   2. gaseous   3. radius   4. years

```
g a s e o u s
r           u
a           i
v           d
i           a
t           r
y e a r s
```

172. 1. Mars   4. meteorites
     2. orbit   5. binary
     3. Ceres

173. 1. eccentric   4. perihelion
     2. ammonia, methane   5. vaporize
     3. Oort   6. nucleus

174. The eight terms are hydrogen, oxygen, liquid, life, clouds, ice, drink, and rain.

175. 1. Meteorites that are four and one-half billion years old have been found.
     2. Large meteorites weigh several tons.
     3. Some meteorites are made of nickel and iron.
     4. Large meteorite craters have been found in Arizona, Canada, and Russia.

176. From left to right: meteors, asteroids, light, Venus, stars, Mercury, moons, Pluto, comets

177. 1. galaxies   4. planets
     2. measure, position   5. celestial
     3. black holes

178. 1. a   4. c
     2. a   5. c
     3. d

179. From top to bottom:
     1. HIKING (line 2)
     2. FISHING (line 3)
     3. NAVIGATION (line 6)

180. 1. Big Dipper   4. nebula
     2. dwarf   5. luminosity
     3. supernova